Native American Mythology
Captivating Myths of Indigenous Peoples from North America

© **Copyright 2019**

All Rights Reserved. No part of this book may be reproduced in any form without permission in writing from the author. Reviewers may quote brief passages in reviews.

Disclaimer: No part of this publication may be reproduced or transmitted in any form or by any means, mechanical or electronic, including photocopying or recording, or by any information storage and retrieval system, or transmitted by email without permission in writing from the publisher.

While all attempts have been made to verify the information provided in this publication, neither the author nor the publisher assumes any responsibility for errors, omissions or contrary interpretations of the subject matter herein.

This book is for entertainment purposes only. The views expressed are those of the author alone and should not be taken as expert instruction or commands. The reader is responsible for his or her own actions.

Adherence to all applicable laws and regulations, including international, federal, state and local laws governing professional licensing, business practices, advertising and all other aspects of doing business in the US, Canada, UK or any other jurisdiction is the sole responsibility of the purchaser or reader.

Neither the author nor the publisher assumes any responsibility or liability whatsoever on the behalf of the purchaser or reader of these materials. Any perceived slight of any individual or organization is purely unintentional.

Free Bonus from Captivating History (Available for a Limited time)

Hi History Lovers!

Now you have a chance to join our exclusive history list so you can get your first history ebook for free as well as discounts and a potential to get more history books for free! Simply visit the link below to join.

Captivatinghistory.com/ebook

Also, make sure to follow us on Facebook, Twitter and Youtube by searching for Captivating History.

Contents

INTRODUCTION 1
PART I: ORIGINS 5
PART II: GHOSTS AND MONSTERS 22
PART III: TRICKSTER TALES 49
PART IV: HERO TALES 67
BIBLIOGRAPHY 89

Introduction

Humans have been living and telling their stories in North America since the end of the last Ice Age. The oldest human artifacts found so far seem to date from around 15,000 years ago. Archeologists have long assumed that the first humans crossed the Bering Strait from Asia much earlier than that and then made their way south and east in bands of hunter-gatherers. Today's Indigenous peoples are the descendants of those early explorers.

However, the story of the peopling of the Americas may not be all that straightforward. Author Craig Childs, in his recent book *Atlas of a Lost World*, says that available evidence indicates a much more complicated picture than the simple Bering Strait story would seem to paint. Childs states that there was more than one migration event, that the initial migrations into the Americas likely followed the coastal water routes then available, and that some migrants might have even come from Europe as well as Asia.

Whatever the real story may have been, what followed from the movements of those Ice-Age hunter-gatherer peoples was a great proliferation of cultures and languages. The myriad cultures and societies that lived in North America for thousands of years before the advent of European explorers and colonists developed their own ways of looking at the world and living within the environments they called home. They also developed sophisticated systems of aquaculture, agriculture, hunting, animal husbandry, and land management according to the resources that were available to them.

Part of the history of Indigenous cultures is, of course, their traditions of storytelling. Myths, legends, and folktales all play important roles in explaining how the world came to be the way it is, as well as giving listeners entertainment with humorous or scary stories, or giving them role models to look up to in hero tales. And I use the word "listeners" purposely, for these stories were first transmitted orally, from teller to listener. For the most part, Indigenous peoples did not use writing to record these tales, and with a very few exceptions, no system of writing seems to have existed for Indigenous languages until after the arrival of white missionaries and colonists.

These storytelling traditions are rich indeed, with thousands upon thousands of stories from hundreds of different cultures. Because of this incredible variety, this book provides but the merest sampling of a broad spectrum of myths and legends, and it makes no claim whatsoever to that sample being representative. That said, I have endeavored to provide at least one myth from every major culture group in North America: Arctic, Subarctic, Plateau, Northwest Coast, Great Basin, Great Plains, California, Southwest, Southeast, and Northeast Forest.

Of the many different genres of story available, I have chosen four for this present volume. The first has to do with the origins of things, either of the world in its entirety or some aspect thereof that was significant to the people who created the story. The other side of creation is death, and so the second section concerns tales of ghosts and monsters, some terrifying, some friendly, some the victims of prank-playing living people. However, out of the acts of destruction wrought by supernatural beings there is often something new created or a change worked that is necessary for the world to function properly.

Tricksters and heroes occupy the third and fourth sections of the book, respectively. Coyote is, of course, a favorite trickster character for most North American Indigenous groups, while Raven is important to peoples in the Pacific Northwest and Arctic regions. Beaver is a trickster for the Nez Perce of the Columbia River Plateau, and for the Pomo of California, little Woodrat also lives by his wits. These tricksters are by turns clever, gullible, victor, and victim, but always there is a moral lesson to be learned from the stories of their adventures.

The final section of the book presents stories of Indigenous heroes. Many of these heroes are shared by multiple cultures, usually within the same or adjacent culture areas. Manabozho, the Menominee hero, is honored by the Ojibwe and many other Algonquin-speaking peoples, who know him as Nanabozho or Nanabush. Glooscap is the favorite hero of the Wabanaki peoples of the northeastern United States and Canadian Maritime provinces. Both Manabozho and Glooscap, in addition to doing the usual heroic things such as fighting monsters and working magic, are powerful beings who also are involved in the creation of the world. Other heroes, such as Blood Clot of the Great Basin and the Great Plains, are beings with supernatural origins but are not themselves creator-beings. Not all heroes are powerful supernatural beings, however: the Hunkpapa Brave Woman may have been an actual historical figure.

But the most important thing about all these stories and the many others told by Indigenous peoples is that they are part of an actual living tradition, not part of a dim and misty past of cultures that no longer exist today. This living tradition shows the resilience of Indigenous cultures, which have survived colonization, the introduction of European diseases, the theft of their lands and resources, and outright acts of genocide on the part of white people and their governments. These stories do tell us something about the past of Indigenous peoples, but they are also very much a part of the Indigenous present and hopefully will also be a part of the future.

Part I: Origins

The Cherokee Creation *(Cherokee, Southeast)*

The Cherokee account of how the world was created is an example of what folklorists call an "earth-diver myth." In these types of myths, a creature or being dives down into the primordial waters and brings up a substance that then is transformed into land, which sets the process of creation in motion. The earth-diver in the myths of some tribes is a turtle, while in others it is a muskrat or a water bird. The Cherokee earth-diver is a water beetle, who goes on a quest on behalf of the other creatures to bring up the bit of mud that becomes the earth.

Whereas in European creation myths a deity or group of deities create the world by the exercise of their power or will, in the Cherokee account the process of creation is begun by the creatures themselves. Insects, animals, and birds all work in concert with the Great Spirit to shape the world and bring it to life, including correcting the Great Spirit's mistake of having placed the sun too close to the ground. Unlike the animals and birds, who existed prior to the world itself, human beings are newcomers and must be created out of nothing by the Great Spirit.

Once there was a time when there was no earth at all. Everything was covered with water, and all the creatures lived in Galunlati, a place that is above the sky. Galunlati was a pleasant place, but soon it became very crowded, and the creatures were unhappy.

"What shall we do?" said the creatures. "There are so many of us, we can barely move."

"I know!" said one of them. "Let's ask Water Beetle to go into the water below and see what he can do about this."

Water Beetle agreed to this plan. He left Galunlati and dove into the waters. He swam around for a bit but didn't see anything that looked like a good place to live, so then he dove deeper. Down, down, down he went, to the bottom of the sea. He picked up a bit of mud in his jaws and brought it up to the surface. When Water Beetle reached the surface with the mud, the mud began to spread out in all directions. The spread-out mud became an island, and the Great Spirit secured it by using cords to tie it to the vault of the sky.

Now, this new island was very good, and it was quite secure, but the ground was too soft for most of the creatures to live on. The creatures decided to send Buzzard down to see whether he might do anything to fix that. Buzzard flew around and around but didn't find anywhere dry enough to land. He flew around some more and finally found one spot that was just dry enough for him to land on. The place where Buzzard landed became the home of the Cherokees, and the flapping of Buzzard's wings as he was landing pushed up the mud in some places and pushed it down in others, forming the hills and mountains and valleys of the world.

Finally the new earth was dry enough for all the creatures to walk on. They came down from the sky vault and looked around their new home. It was solid enough, but it was very dark. The creatures didn't like the darkness, so they invited Sun to come down and join them. She came and agreed to walk a particular path every day to give light to the new world.

Everyone except Crawfish was happy about the light Sun gave. It was much too hot for him. "Look at my beautiful shell!" he cried. "Look! It's turned bright red because Sun is too hot. Can anyone help me?"

The creatures took pity on Crawfish and raised Sun a little higher. It was still too hot. So they raised Sun a bit more. It was still too hot. Seven times they pushed Sun a little farther up in the sky. After the seventh time, Sun was finally in the right spot.

Now that there was land and water and light, the Great Spirit decided to make plants to grow on the new land. When all the plants were made, he told them and all the animals that they should stay awake for seven whole days. The animals tried their best, but the only one who was able to stay awake the whole time was Owl. Because he succeeded, the Great Spirit gave Owl the power of seeing in the dark. The plants also tried, but only the pines, firs, holly, and some others were able to stay awake the whole time. The Great Spirit gave them the gift of keeping their leaves all year round.

Once all the plants were made, the Great Spirit decided that there should be people in the world. The Great Spirit made a man and a woman. When man and woman were first created, they did not know how to make children in the usual way. The first time they made children, the man took a fish and pushed it against the woman's belly. Then the woman gave birth to a child. They did this every seven days. After the seventh day, the Great Spirit thought that that was enough for now, and he made it so that women could only have a child once a year.

The Good Twin and the Evil Twin *(Yuma, Southwest)*

The creation myth of the Yuma people of Arizona is very different from the Cherokee story. In the Yuma account, the creator is a supernatural dual being, having good and evil aspects. This being arises out of the primordial waters in its good aspect first, and when the evil aspect tries to rise, the good aspect ensures that it is blinded in order to limit its power.

This version of the myth was collected after the advent of Europeans into Yuma territory. The Yuma creation story not only explains how people came to be but also attributes the creation of separate cultures to Kokomaht, the All-Father who is the primary creator of the world. Once the Yuma encountered white people, they apparently thought it necessary to incorporate them into their creation myth.

What the Yuma have to say about Europeans is not flattering, and considering the history of the behavior of whites toward Indigenous peoples, this is neither surprising nor unreasonable. The white people that figure in this story are painted as selfish, greedy, vain, and petulant, and as interlopers unfit for survival in the desert environment that the Yuma inhabit, the environment for which the Yuma believe they were specially made by Kokomaht.

In the very beginning, the only thing in existence was water. The sky had not yet been made. The earth had not yet been made. There were no plants or animals or fish or people. The sky was made when the waters swirled and swirled about and made foam and spray. The foam and spray rose up, up, up, and turned into the sky.

Down at the very bottom of the waters, there was a being that was one and two at the same time, and the two were twins. The being's name was Kokomaht, which means All-Father.

A second time the waters swirled about. They crashed and thundered in great waves. Again the crashing and swirling of the waters made foam and spray. Up from the depths a being arose. It rose up through the waters with its eyes closed and pushed through the surface. Then it stood upon the surface of the waters and looked about. The being called itself Kokomaht, and Kokomaht was a good being.

As Kokomaht looked over the waters and up in the sky, he heard a voice calling to him from the depths. The voice said, "My brother! When you rose to the surface, did you keep your eyes open or closed?"

Now, Kokomaht knew that the voice belonged to his brother, and that his brother had an evil nature. Kokomaht wanted to make sure that his brother could work as little evil as possible, so he lied and said, "Oh, I kept my eyes open the whole way!"

The evil twin believed what Kokomaht said. He kept his eyes open as he rose to the surface, but in doing so, he blinded himself. Kokomaht named his twin "Bakotahl," which means "Blind One."

Kokomaht decided that it was time to create the earth. First, he created the four directions. He took four steps in one direction, stopped, pointed in the direction he had been going, and then said, "This is north." Then he went back to the center again. Kokomaht turned around and went the opposite way. He took four steps, pointed, and said, "This is south." He returned to the center, and in the same way he created east and west.

"It is now time to make the earth," said Kokomaht, but Bakotahl objected.

"I should be the one to make the earth," said Bakotahl.

"No, I am going to do it," said Kokomaht, and so he put his hand into the waters and began stirring. Kokomaht stirred and stirred the waters, and soon they became so agitated that a great mass of land came to the surface. Kokomaht went onto the new land and sat down.

Bakotahl was angry and envious that his brother got to make the earth, but he kept his feelings to himself. Bakotahl also climbed onto the new land and sat down next to Kokomaht. Bakotahl thought to himself, "If I am not to be allowed to make the land, then I shall make some people to live on it."

Bakotahl took up a handful of mud and started forming it into a creature. Bakotahl gave the creature a head and a body. He gave it arms and legs. But he forgot to put fingers and toes on the hands. Bakotahl's new creature was lumpy and imperfect, and so Bakotahl was ashamed of it and hid it from his brother.

Kokomaht then said, "I think I shall make some people to walk on this new land." Kokomaht took up a handful of mud and shaped it into a being. He gave it a head and a body. He gave it arms and legs. He put fingers and toes on the hands and feet, and gave the being a beautiful face. Everything about Kokomaht's new being was perfect.

When the being was all made, Kokomaht took it and waved it four times toward the north. Kokomaht then set the new being down upon the new land, and the being came alive. It stood on its feet and walked around. It could see and hear and taste and smell. This being was the first man. Then Kokomaht took up another handful of mud and made a woman the same way he had made the man.

Bakotahl made another attempt at making people. When he had made seven of his lumpy, imperfect creatures, Kokomaht asked him what he was making.

"I am making people," said Bakotahl.

"Hm," said Kokomaht. "I think they're missing some important things. Here, feel the people I made. They have fingers and toes and features on their faces. Yours are lumpy and misshapen. They won't be able to care for themselves or each other." Then Kokomaht took his foot and kicked Bakotahl's new beings into the water.

When Bakotahl learned what Kokomaht had done, he became terribly angry. Bakotahl dove into the water and swam down, down, down into the depths. Bakotahl made the waters swirl and heave, and up out of the depths he sent a whirlwind. Kokomaht saw the whirlwind, and when it got near enough, he stepped on it and crushed it to death. But not all of the whirlwind was crushed; one little piece escaped from beneath Kokomaht's foot, and this is where all sicknesses come from.

Now all there was on the new land was Kokomaht and the new man and the new woman, and they were the first Yumas. Kokomaht made more men and more women. He put them in pairs, and each pair became the first ones of new tribes, the Cocopahs, Digueños, and

Mojaves. Now that Kokomaht had made four pairs of people, he rested a while. When he was done with his rest, Kokomaht made the first men and first women for the Apaches, the Maricopas, the Pimas, and the Coahuilas. In this way, Kokomaht made the first men and first women for twenty-four tribes of people. The white people were the last ones he made.

The Yuma man said to Kokomaht, "We don't know how to live in this new place. Please teach us."

"First you must learn about children," said Kokomaht, and so he made a son for himself and called him Komashtam'ho. Then Kokomaht said to the people, "Men and women should live together and have children together."

Kokomaht looked at the sky and the land and the people he had made. These were all good things, but he felt that his creation was incomplete. "I know!" said Kokomaht. "My new people will need light."

Kokomaht then created the moon and the morning star. Then he made all the other stars that shine at night. When this was done, Kokomaht looked at all the new things he had made and said, "I think I have created enough. My son can make more new things if he wants to."

In addition to the land and the people and the moon and the stars, Kokomaht had created some other beings. One of these was Hanyi, the Frog. Hanyi was very jealous of Kokomaht's power and would have liked nothing better than to destroy him. Of course Kokomaht knew what was in Hanyi's heart because he knew the thoughts of all the beings he created. Kokomaht thought, "I have one last lesson to teach my new beings, and I will have Hanyi help me. I must teach the people how to die. I will let Hanyi kill me."

Hanyi decided the time had come for her to try to kill Kokomaht. She burrowed into the earth beneath Kokomaht's feet and sucked all his breath out through a hole in the earth that was there. When Hanyi had taken all of Kokomaht's breath, Kokomaht became very sick. He lay down on the earth. He called all the new people he had made to come and watch how to die. Everyone came except the white man. He stayed in his own country in the west of the world.

Now, the white man was very unhappy and dissatisfied with everything. He was also very greedy, taking what didn't belong to him without asking. One day, the white man sat crying because he didn't like his curly, pale hair and pale skin. Komashtam'ho was tired of listening to the white man feeling sorry for himself, so he took two sticks and tied them together into a cross. He gave the sticks to the white man. "Here," said Komashtam'ho. "Take these. You can ride on them. Just stop whining." The white man took the sticks and straddled them. The sticks turned into a horse, and for a while the white man stopped crying and complaining.

Kokomaht lay on the ground, where he was deathly ill. He said to the people, "This is the last thing I will teach you. I will teach you how to die." After he finished speaking, Kokomaht died.

When Kokomaht was dead, Komashtam'ho began to think of what he would like to create for this new world his father had made. He thought that maybe it would be good to have both night and day, so he spat into his hand and made a disk out of the spittle. Komashtam'ho took the disk and threw it into the east, where it began to shine. Now the world had a sun as well as a moon and stars.

Komashtam'ho explained to the people that the sun would move from east to west and that there now would be day and night. To show them how this would be, he took the sun and pushed it under the earth, making everything dark again. While it was dark, Komashtam'ho made some more stars and put them into the sky. "When the sun is out, it will be day, and there will be much light. You will not be able to see the stars. When the sun sets in the west, it will be night, and it will be dark again. You will be able to see the stars."

When the sun had been made, Komashtam'ho thought about what he should do with his father's body. He decided that the best thing would be to burn it on a pyre, but there was nothing on the new earth that would burn, so Komashtam'ho made wood. He heaped the wood into a large pyre and put his father's body on top of it.

Now, Komashtam'ho knew that Coyote was likely to try some kind of a trick with his father's body, so he gave Coyote a stick and told him to go fetch fire from the sun. When Coyote had run away, Komashtam'ho showed the people how to make their own fire using a piece of wood with a hole in it and another stick. Komashtam'ho put one end of the stick into the hole and twirled it between his hands until a small flame licked up. This is how the people learned how to make fire. Then Komashtam'ho took the flame and used it to light the funeral pyre.

The people all gathered around the pyre and watched it burn, but they did not mourn for Kokomaht because they didn't yet understand that death was forever. As the pyre was beginning to burn, Coyote returned. He jumped over all the people onto the pyre, where he took the heart of Kokomaht in his jaws and ate it before running away.

Komashtam'ho was very angry at Coyote. "You will be cursed for that!" he shouted. "You will always live in the wilderness, and you will be a thief. Everyone will shun you and kill you when they can."

Then Komashtam'ho turned to the people and said, "Now you know about death. Kokomaht will never be among you ever again, for death must be for always. If there was no death, there would be too many creatures in the world, and there wouldn't be enough food."

When the people heard that Kokomaht would never return, they began to weep, for now they understood that death was for always. And because the flames of Kokomaht's pyre were so very hot, it made the whole land hot ever after. Hanyi the Frog watched the people mourning for Kokomaht and understood that they would be very angry with her for killing him. So Hanyi buried herself in a burrow underground, and that is why frogs still live in those burrows to this day.

Komashtam'ho saw the people weeping, and he said to them, "You will mourn now, and that is fitting, but when you die, your spirits will go to the place where Kokomaht is. There you will always be happy, as he is happy now."

Then Komashtam'ho decided he needed help with creating the rest of the world. He chose a man named Marhokuvek to help him. Marhokuvek looked at the people and creatures mourning for Kokomaht and saw that they were all covered with long hair, for people and animals and birds did not look all that different from one another when the world was first made. Marhokuvek said, "Let us cut our hair as a sign that we are in mourning."

The people and animals and birds thought this was a good idea, and so they cut off all their hair, but when Komashtam'ho saw what the animals and birds looked like without their hair, he said, "The people look all right without hair, but the animals and birds do not." So Komashtam'ho changed the forms of the animals and birds into the shapes they have now, and gave hair to the animals and feathers to the birds. Then Komashtam'ho realized that some of the animals and birds were very wild and dangerous indeed, so he sent a great rain to wash these away. It rained and it rained and it rained, and soon the whole world was flooding. The flood washed away many of the dangerous animals, but it also began to kill some of the good animals and people as well, and the air became very cold.

"Please stop the flood!" said Marhokuvek. "You are killing people and good animals, and the people cannot live in such a cold world!"

Komashtam'ho agreed to stop the rain, but from that day forward, the animals, birds, and people lived separately, and the animals and birds were afraid of the people. To dry up all the floodwaters, Komashtam'ho kindled a great fire, which burned all the land. This is why the home of the Yuma people is a desert.

Now, the body of Kokomaht had been well destroyed in the flames, but his house was still standing, with all his belongings inside. Komashtam'ho said to the people, "We shouldn't leave Kokomaht's house standing because he is dead now, and every time we see his house or his belongings, it will make us sad. So when someone dies, we have to destroy their house and their belongings."

Komashtam'ho went to his father's house and used a long pole to knock it down. Then he used the pole to dig up the place where the house had been. Water began to well up from the ground in the places that Komashtam'ho had dug into the soil, and the grooves made by the pole filled with the water and became the Colorado River.

Now, the people that Bakotahl had made had not been completely destroyed. They still lived, although they had neither hands nor feet, nor fingers nor toes. Some of these beings became the fish and other creatures who live in the water, while others turned into waterfowl.

After all had been created, the different kinds of people parted from one another and went to live in different places. Komashtam'ho said to the Yuma people, "I have finished creating the world. I will always be with you, but I must change my form because I will also need to be with other people as well. And in my new form, you must call me by a new name. I shall be Eshpahkomahl, the White Eagle."

Then Komashtam'ho changed himself into four eagles. One was black and flew to the west; this is where dark clouds and rain come from. One was brown and went to the south and flew over the rivers to catch fish. No one knows what the third eagle looks like, for no one has ever seen him. Komashtam'ho himself flew to the north in the form of a white eagle.

And Bakotahl? He still lives under the earth and still has an evil heart. Sometimes the earth shakes, and the people say that it is Bakotahl moving about in his underground home.

Pushing up the Sky *(Snohomish, Northwest Coast)*

The Snohomish people of Puget Sound acknowledge a single creator who makes the world, and although the creator does a good job, he neglects to make the sky high enough, so the people and animals have to fix the problem. This legend therefore functions as a just-so story about why the sky is so far away and about why it is so difficult to get into the Sky World, a mythical region above the earth that contains the stars.

According to the Snohomish myth, in the beginning it was easy for people and animals to go into the Sky World because the sky was so low and actually touched the earth at the horizon. The permeable nature of the earth/sky boundary factors into another just-so aspect of this tale, which explains the origin of the constellations of the Big and Little Dippers. These two constellations are formed when some hunters and fishermen accidentally cross the earth/sky boundary during the sky-pushing and end up caught in the Sky World, where they turn into stars.

The retelling below is based on a version of the legend told by Snohomish Chief William Shelton.

The Creator and Changer made the whole world. He started in the east and worked his way westward. He created the land and the waters, the birds and the beasts, and the people. He gave all the creatures their places to live, and he gave languages to the people. When he had made the land from the east all the way to Puget Sound, and when he had put all the people and all the creatures in their places, he saw that he still had many, many languages left to give. So he scattered them all around Puget Sound and the lands to the north, and so it was that the people who lived in that part of the world spoke many, many different languages and could not always understand one another.

The people all had good places to live, but there was one thing about the world they did not like. The Creator hadn't put the sky up high enough, and the tall people were always bumping their heads on it. There was also a second problem: if a person climbed high enough into a tall tree, they could enter the Sky World, and they often didn't come back.

Finally the elders of the tribes got together to see whether they could figure out what to do about the sky being so low. After talking for a long time, they agreed that somehow they needed to push the sky up higher.

"This will take all of us working together," said one very wise elder. "All the people and all the birds and all the animals will have to push at the same time."

"This is a good plan," said another elder, "but how will we make sure everyone works together like that? We speak too many languages, and we need one signal everyone will understand."

"I know what we can do!" said a third elder. "Let's all push when someone shouts 'Ya-hoh.' That word is the same in all our languages, and it means 'let's push together.'"

The elders all agreed that this was a very good plan. They sent messengers throughout the whole land, telling the people and the birds and the animals what they were going to do, and setting a day for them to push up the sky. The messengers also told the people to take the trunks of fir trees and fit them to use as poles to push the sky up.

The people worked very hard making the poles. Finally the day to push up the sky arrived. The people raised their poles, set them against the sky, and got ready to push. When everyone was in place, the elders all cried, "Ya-hoh!" and the people pushed on the sky with their poles. The sky moved a little bit. So, the elders cried, "Ya-hoh!" again, and the people pushed again, and the sky moved up a little bit more. The people worked and worked this way for a long time. The elders would cry, "Ya-hoh!" and everyone would push, and finally, after much effort, they had put the sky where it is now. The tall people were much happier because they were no longer bumping their heads all the time. And since the day of the sky-pushing, no one has been able to climb high enough to get into the Sky World.

Now, not everyone had heard about the sky-pushing. There were three hunters who had been out chasing four elk and so were away from the rest of the people when the messengers came. They chased and chased the elk for several days. On the day set for the sky-pushing but before the people had begun their work with their poles, the hunters and their prey came to the place where the sky met the earth. The elk jumped into the Sky World, and the hunters followed them, but when the people lifted up the sky, the elk and the hunters went up with it, along with their dog.

The elk, the dog, and the hunters could not leave the Sky World, and there they turned into stars. You can still see them there even today. The three hunters form the handle of the Big Dipper, and you can see the dog as a very small star next to the bigger one in the middle of the handle. The elk form the bowl of the Big Dipper.

The hunters were not the only ones that got caught in the sky that day. There were two canoes with three fishermen each that were out fishing. They got caught up in the sky when it lifted, too, along with a fish, and they also were all turned into stars, and became the Little Dipper.

And to this day, the people who live in Puget Sound still shout "Ya-hoh!" when they have to do a difficult task together.

The Origin of El Capitan *(Miwok, California)*

El Capitan is an enormous granite monolith on the north side of the Yosemite Valley in California. In this story of how El Capitan came to be, told by the Miwok people of central California, there is no direct action by a supernatural being, just a random occurrence that results in an otherwise unremarkable large, flat rock suddenly growing overnight into something the size of a mountain.

One of the primary features of El Capitan is the nearly sheer vertical surface of its face, which is scalable only by a few of the most skilled climbers. The difficulty inherent in climbing El Capitan therefore figures largely in this story, which begins when a family of bears is stranded at the top of the monolith when it grows under them during the night. As soon as the other animals discover what has happened to the bears, they rush to launch a rescue mission to get the bears down. However, none of the animals are able to climb very high up the cliff face, no matter how hard they try, until finally the lowly inchworm, who can cling to just about anything, offers to go. The inchworm does make it to the top, but not before the bears have died from starvation.

The sheerness of the cliff face and the idea that nothing but a clingy worm might be able to climb it factors into the Miwok name for El Capitan: Tutokanula, *or "Inchworm Stone."*

There was a time when a mother bear and her two cubs spent the day along the Merced River looking for food. They had walked and foraged for a very long time, and they were very tired. They walked a little farther, looking for a place to rest. Soon they came upon a large, flat rock that was big enough for all of them to lie down on. The bears climbed up on the rock, curled up, and went to sleep.

The bears slept soundly on the rock all night. They slept so soundly that they did not notice the rock growing and growing under them while they slept. The rock grew so much, that when the bears woke in the morning, they found they could touch the moon. The bears were very frightened. They looked over the edge of the rock. All they saw was the sheer edge of the cliff face. No matter which way they looked, they could not find a way back down to the valley.

The bears were not the only ones who were surprised by what happened. The birds and animals of the Yosemite Valley looked up in shock when they found that the flat rock at the side of the river was now as big as a mountain. The birds and animals also heard the cries of the mother bear and her cubs, and they saw the bears peering cautiously over the edge of the great rock.

All the animals and birds were very worried about the bear and her cubs. "How are we to get them down?" they said. "There's no food up there. If we don't rescue those bears, they will starve!"

So the animals and birds came together in a great council to determine what was to be done. In the end, they decided that someone needed to climb up to the bears and help them get down.

"I'll go!" said Mouse, and he scampered off to the rescue. But try as he might, little Mouse was unable to climb very far up the steep sides of the giant rock.

Next Rat said that he would go, but he had no more success than Mouse had done, although he was able to climb just a bit higher. Rabbit went next and got a little higher than Rat had done, but he came nowhere near the top. Then Mountain Lion tried, and Fox, and Crow, and many other creatures after them, but none of them were able to climb high enough to help the bears.

Soon all the animals and birds despaired of being able to help the bears. Finally, little Inchworm came forward. "I may be very small," he said, "but I'm a very good climber."

And so Inchworm inched off to the foot of the great rock and began to climb. Slowly and carefully he made his way up the steep face of the cliff. He passed the place where Mouse had had to stop. Then he passed the place that Rat had reached. Then he passed the places that Mountain Lion, Fox, and Crow had reached. Soon Inchworm had passed the places that all the other animals had been able to climb to, and still he kept climbing on and on.

It took a very long time for Inchworm to reach the top of the huge cliff, but finally he arrived. Unfortunately, because it had taken so long for anyone to come to the rescue, the bears had starved to death by the time Inchworm arrived. Inchworm gathered up the bones and brought them down to where the other animals were waiting. Everyone was very sad that the bears had died, and they put the bones to rest in the traditional way.

And this is why the mountain that white people call "El Capitan" is called "Tutokanula" by the Miwoks, because that word means "Inchworm Stone" in their language.

Part II: Ghosts and Monsters

Burnt-Stick and the Wendigo *(Sweet Grass Cree, Subarctic)*

The wendigo is a fearsome two-faced giant with a taste for human flesh who appears in stories from Algonquin and Dene tribes. In this story from the Sweet Grass Cree of Saskatchewan, Canada, we learn that the wendigo is so dangerous that even Wisahketchahk, the main Algonquin culture hero, is afraid of it.

Here a girl named Burnt-Stick comes to live with eleven brothers who have escaped the wendigo and who are also accompanied by Wisahketchahk. But Burnt-Stick is no ordinary girl; from the very moment of her arrival, it is clear she has supernatural origins. Her capture by the wendigo—which she escapes with the help of the creature's grandmother—is what eventually leads to the wendigo being soundly killed by a young man who also seems to be a supernatural being.

Burnt-Stick lives with the young man and his wife for a time, and there she assumes male clothing and goes hunting as though she were a man. This cross-dressing later saves her from being pounced on by an evil man who likes to dive out of trees onto unsuspecting women to maim or kill them. Of course Burnt-Stick goes on to give the evil man his just deserts, and returns to her brothers with some of the young women she saved to be their wives, thus undoing some of the wendigo's evil by making it possible to increase the population.

The retelling presented below is based on the story told by the Cree storyteller Louis Moosimin to Canadian anthropologist Leonard Bloomfield in the early 20th century.

Once there was a dreadful wendigo who had made it his task to destroy every human being in the world. He attacked encampment after encampment, killing and eating as many people as he could. After one attack, ten young men managed to escape together. When the wendigo found out they had escaped, he chased after them, but they always managed to find a new place to camp and to leave before the wendigo could catch them.

The young men had fled so quickly that they had left their little brother behind. They went back to get their little brother and then moved on. The young men and their little brother found a good place to set up their encampment. It was a good place that seemed safe from the wendigo. While the elder brothers did the hunting and other tasks that men do, the younger brother stayed in the lodge and did things like tend the fire.

One day, as the younger brother was tending the fire, he stepped on a piece of wood. He found that a splinter had pierced the skin of his sole. The young boy pulled the splinter out of his foot and then threw it out the door of the lodge. No sooner had he done that than a little girl-child came crawling in. "Oh no you don't," said the young boy. "I don't know how to take care of a girl, and neither do my brothers." And so he took the girl-child and put her back outside the lodge.

Not a moment later, the girl-child came back in. She was much bigger than she had been before, but again the young boy put her back outside. Another time the girl came in, and this time she looked at the boy and said, "Big brother!" to him. The boy set her outside yet again, thinking to himself, "Maybe when she comes back next time, she will be all grown up. If she has been sent to us by the spirits, then she will be grown up, and she can stay with us."

Sure enough, the girl came back, and this time she had grown into a young woman. "Come in and sit down, Big Sister!" said the young boy, and so she came into the lodge. The young boy gave her the name Burnt-Stick. The boy introduced Burnt-Stick to his brothers, and they were glad to have her join them to do the work that women usually do.

Now, at this time, Wisahketchahk was also staying with the ten young men, and he was with them because he was terribly frightened. The wendigo was such a fearsome beast that even Wisahketchahk ran from him. Wisahketchahk stayed with the young men because they knew much about the ways of the wendigo, how it hunted and which paths it walked. When Wisahketchahk met Burnt-Stick, he said, "Welcome, Little Sister!" and it was then that the young men and their little brother knew that it was right for Burnt-Stick to stay with them.

And so this little band lived together and worked together. The men hunted and fished and did all the work that men usually do, while Burnt-Stick tanned hides and sewed clothing and cooked and did all the work that women usually do, and for a time they were all very happy together in that place.

One day, Wisahketchahk said to Burnt-Stick, "We have been here for some time. The wendigo probably knows where we are. But your brothers and I need to go away for a few days, and you must stay here by yourself. If you do what I tell you, you will be safe.

"First, you must go out and collect enough firewood to last you four nights. Whenever you are gathering firewood from now on, do not pick up anything else but the wood. While we are not at home, you might hear someone calling to you, but you must not answer. For the four nights we will be away, it will be very cold. You might hear what sounds like our voices outside the lodge, but it will not be us. You must stay inside and not open the door. The wendigo is sure to be abroad while we are away, and he has such great power that even I am afraid of him."

The young woman followed Wisahketchahk's advice. She went into the forest and gathered a lot of wood for the fire. She also cut down a tree and split the wood to use as well. She put all the firewood inside the lodge and sealed the door because the weather had become very, very cold.

After a little while, she heard someone say, "Little Sister, we have returned!" but Burnt-Stick remembered what Wisahketchahk had told her. She didn't answer, and she didn't open the door. Then she heard what sounded like her brothers suffering from the cold. "We are dying!" the voices said. "We are dying from the cold! Open the door, and let us in!" Burnt-Stick didn't open the door, and in the morning when she went outside, there were no footprints at all. "Wisahketchahk was right!" she thought. "The wendigo did come last night, and he tried to trick me!"

After four nights, the men came back to the lodge. Burnt-Stick had followed Wisahketchahk's instructions and had stayed safe the whole time. The morning after the men came home, Burnt-Stick went to collect wood for the fire. But this time she forgot Wisahketchahk's warning, and she picked up a pretty feather she found on the forest floor. Suddenly, the wendigo came out of the feather, saying, "Aha! I have you at last. You are young and tender, and you shall make a tasty dish for me when you have been properly fattened." Then the wendigo picked up Burnt-Stick, threw her over his shoulder, and strode back to his home.

Now, the wendigo lived with his old grandmother, and it was she who cooked the people that he brought home to eat. When the wendigo arrived home with Burnt-Stick, he put the girl down and said, "Hey, Grandmother! Look at this tasty morsel I found. Fatten her up nicely for me, for I intend to feast on her when she is ready."

For a time Burnt-Stick lived with the wendigo and his grandmother. Then came the day when the wendigo decided that he would eat

Burnt-Stick. He told his grandmother to kill the girl and cook her, and then he went out.

The grandmother did not want to kill Burnt-Stick because she had become fond of the young girl. The grandmother went to Burnt-Stick and said, "Grandchild, the wendigo wants me to kill you so that he can eat you, but I don't want to do that. I have already had a long life; take that axe there, and kill me by striking me in the head with it, and then put me in the pot instead. When you have done that, run far away from here. Go in that direction when you leave. You will see four hills in front of you. You must climb each one of those. When you have crossed the hills, you will find an iron house. Knock on the door of that house, and ask for help. The one who lives there can kill the wendigo. Say to the one who lives there, 'Big Brother! Help me! The wendigo wants to eat me!' and then you will have good help."

When the grandmother was done instructing Burnt-Stick, the young woman took the axe and killed her. Then she skinned the grandmother, cut her up, and set her in a kettle over the stove to cook. As soon as the meal was done cooking, Burnt-Stick ran out of the wendigo's house in the direction the grandmother had told her to go. Burnt-Stick came across the first hill. She climbed up one side and down the other. Then she came to the second hill, and she climbed that one as well. But as she began to climb the third hill, she heard the roaring voice of the wendigo behind her. The wendigo had discovered that he had eaten his grandmother instead of having eaten Burnt-Stick, and he was very angry. "You will never get away from me!" roared the wendigo. "I will follow you everywhere, and I will surely find you and eat you!"

Burnt-Stick began to run even faster. She went down the third hill and climbed up the fourth. As she crested that hill, she looked behind her, and there in the distance was the wendigo, running as fast as he could to catch her. Then Burnt-Stick looked down in front of her, and there was the iron house as the grandmother had told her. She ran as fast as she could and then began pounding on the door and shouting, "Please, oh please let me in! The wendigo is chasing me!"

But these were not the words the grandmother had told Burnt-Stick to use, so the people inside the house did not open the door. Finally Burnt-Stick remembered what she had to say. "Big Brother! Help me! The wendigo wants to eat me!"

As soon as Burnt-Stick said those words, the door opened, and she went inside the house. Inside there were a young man and a young woman. The young woman said to Burnt-Stick, "Sister-in-law, welcome! Please come sit down!"

No sooner had Burnt-Stick sat down than they heard the wendigo roaring its way around the house. "Open this door!" screamed the wendigo. "Open this door, and let me in! I mean to have that girl for my dinner! Open up!"

The young man took up his axe and opened the door. As soon as the wendigo stuck its head in, the young man swung the axe and chopped off the wendigo's head.

The young man and young woman welcomed Burnt-Stick into their home. She lived with them for some time. The young man and young woman made a talisman for Burnt-Stick to carry with her. "This will give you manitou power," they said. They also made men's clothing for Burnt-Stick to wear, and dressed as a man, she went out hunting every day.

One day, the young man and young woman said to Burnt-Stick, "Your brothers miss you. You really should go visit them. But on your way home, take care; there is an evil man who lives in a huge tipi. He likes to climb up into trees and jump down upon the people who pass by. Every time he lands on someone, he breaks their bones. Sometimes he even kills them. Now, he will not try to kill you if you are dressed like a man; he only jumps on women. But maybe you can do something about that evil man when you come across him."

Burnt-Stick began her journey homeward. She tried to avoid the evil man's camp, but he had seen her approaching from afar and met her on the trail. Thinking Burnt-Stick was a man, the evil one said, "Come and enjoy hospitality at my lodge." Burnt-Stick couldn't refuse for fear of raising his suspicions.

They walked on for a time, and slowly it dawned on the evil man that Burnt-Stick was, in fact, a woman and not a man. He made a plan to jump on her out of a tree but not before he had frightened her by showing her all the young women whose bones he had broken whom he forced to live with him. Burnt-Stick sensed that the evil man had discovered who she really was, so she picked up a long piece of saskatoon wood and pretended she needed it for a walking stick.

The evil man led Burnt-Stick into his lodge, and there she saw the broken bodies of all the women he had harmed. Burnt-Stick felt sorrow and anger for them, and she vowed to stop the evil man from hurting anyone else.

"Come and sit here," said the evil one, and Burnt-Stick took the seat she was offered. Then the evil one went out of the lodge to climb his tree and wait for Burnt-Stick to come looking for him. After the man had been gone for a little while, Burnt-Stick held up her walking stick and said, "Walking stick, turn yourself into iron, and let that evil man impale himself upon you!"

The stick turned into iron, and so Burnt-Stick went to the tree where the evil man had hidden himself. Thinking that his plan had worked, the man leaped out of the tree at Burnt-Stick. But she held out the iron rod she had made out of the saskatoon walking stick, and the evil man was impaled upon it and died.

Burnt-Stick went back to the evil one's lodge. She healed all the women who had broken bodies, and she restored the dead ones to life. Selecting ten of the women to accompany her, Burnt-Stick finished her journey toward her brothers' house. When she arrived there, she found all her brothers in mourning. "Oh, oh, oh!" they cried. "The wendigo has eaten our little sister! The wendigo has eaten Burnt-Stick!"

Burnt-Stick stood before her brothers and said, "Do not mourn! I am here! The wendigo has not eaten me!"

The brothers rejoiced greatly that their sister was still alive. They listened in wonder as she told them her tale. Then she introduced the ten women she brought with her, "These women I saved from the evil one, and they have consented to be wives to you." Burnt-Stick's brothers married the women, and they were very happy together.

Not many days after the weddings, Burnt-Stick stood before her family and said, "I must leave you now. I am not a human being. I hear my father calling me back to him. I will turn into a deer, and in that form I shall leave you, since I have finished the work I was sent here to do."

The Double-Faced Ghost *(Cheyenne, Great Plains)*

A giant, two-faced supernatural creature also appears in this story from the Cheyenne people of the Great Plains. Unlike his wendigo counterpart, however, the Cheyenne ghost is not dangerous at all. He is generous, kind, and gracious, but most importantly, he is lonely and in want of a wife.

Once the ghost finds a woman he wants to marry, he goes out of his way to show the family that he is a good person. The family is, of course, quite frightened once they discover that a ghost has been helping them, but they treat the ghost with respect, and the father finds a way to honorably deny the ghost his daughter's hand without making the ghost lose face.

The game that the father plays with the ghost is called "hide-the-plum-pit" in the sources consulted for this book, but from the description of the game in the story, it would seem to be some version of the moccasin game, which was enjoyed by many Indigenous peoples, including Plains Indians such as the Cheyenne. The game uses three or four moccasins and a small object such as a pebble or a plum pit. One player hides the object under or inside one of the moccasins while using sleight of hand to disguise where the object is actually hidden, and the other player has to guess in which moccasin the object has been placed.

Once there was a ghost who was extremely tall. His legs were so long that he could cross a river in one stride or hop from hilltop to hilltop with no effort at all. His arms were long to match his legs, which made it very easy for him to catch any game he cared to hunt. But his height and his arms and his legs were not the oddest things about this ghost. No, his strangest feature was that his head had two faces, one facing front and the other looking behind, and so his name was Double-Face.

Double-Face liked that he could stride across rivers and over hills with great ease. He liked that he was a good hunter. And yet he was not happy because he had no wife, and of course being a ghost made it even more difficult for him to find a woman who might marry him.

One fine, sunny day, Double-Face decided to take a good long walk across the prairie. He strode along, feeling sad that he had no wife and wondering what he might do about his plight, when suddenly he saw a tipi off in the distance. The tipi was all by itself; there were no other tipis or people anywhere around it for miles. The ghost decided to go closer and see who lived in the tipi. Maybe there was even a woman who might consent to marry him!

The ghost crept as close to the tipi as he dared and then hid himself behind a convenient hill. He saw that three people lived in the tipi: a man, his wife, and their daughter. The ghost watched as the people went about their business, and as soon as he caught sight of the young woman, he knew he had found his bride. The young woman was so very beautiful, and the ghost could not wait to have her for his wife. But how to convince the family to let him marry her? It was unlikely that a living human girl would want a ghost for a husband, and her parents likely would not be happy with a ghost for a son-in-law. The ghost thought and thought about what he might do to convince the family that he would make a good husband for the young woman, and then he had an idea: he was a very good hunter, so he would bring the family fresh meat every day and leave it at the door of their tipi. Once they realized that he meant them no harm and would be a good provider, surely they would let him marry the young woman!

Pleased with his plan, the ghost set about to hunting, and soon he had caught a great deal of game. He dressed it, and just before daybreak, he left it on a clean antelope skin just outside the tipi. Then the ghost went and hid behind the hill to see what the people would do. When the sun came up, the people came out of the tipi and saw the great pile of meat the ghost had left. They were very happy to see that someone had given them this gift, but they were also puzzled. They looked around and called out their thanks to whoever had left them the meat, but when they saw no one and no one answered, they set about cooking and eating some of the meat and preserving the rest of it for another time.

This went on for several days. The ghost would go hunting and catch a lot of fat game, and then leave it in front of the tipi just before daybreak. Then the people would come out and try to find their benefactor, but since the ghost stayed well hidden, they never understood who would be so kind and generous to them.

Finally, the father had had enough of the mystery. "I am going to find out who it is that leaves us this fine game every morning," he said. "We really need to thank them, and I am tired of the mystery."

The father went a little way away from the tipi and dug a hole just large enough for him to hide in. Once it was dark, he got in the hole and waited. For a long time, nothing happened, and it was hard for him to stay awake. But just before dawn, the father saw something coming toward the tipi. It was incredibly tall and was carrying a bundle of game in its enormously long arms. Once the creature got close to the tipi, it left the game outside the door and strode away.

That was when the father realized that the thing not only was a giant, but it also had two faces!

Once he thought it safe to do so, the father climbed out of the hole and ran into the tipi. "Wake up! Wake up!" he shouted to his wife and daughter. "Wake up! We must pack up our things and leave! I saw who has been leaving the meat. It's a huge ghost or monster or something, taller than the tallest tree, and it has two faces, one in front and one behind! We mustn't stay here a moment longer!"

The family hurriedly struck the tipi and packed up their belongings. They walked and walked all day, not daring to stop except to drink a little water and eat a little food. They wanted to get as far away from the monster as they could.

Sometime after the family had departed, Double-Face came back to the place where the tipi had stood to see whether the family had accepted his latest gift. There he found the meat lying on the antelope skin, but the tipi was gone. Double-Face looked at the ground and saw the family's tracks. He followed the tracks, and with long strides of his long legs, he caught up to them in no time. He stepped in front of them and said, "Wait! Please don't run away! I'm not going to hurt you! Won't you please listen to me?"

The family realized they had no way of escaping a monster who could cross a river in one stride or hop from hilltop to hilltop, so they stopped. The father said, "We are grateful for all the meat you left for us. We will listen to you. Tell us what it is you want."

"One day as I was striding across the prairie, I was feeling sorry for myself because I don't have a wife. Then I saw your tipi, and I saw your beautiful daughter, and I fell in love with her. I left you the meat because I want her to be my wife, and I wanted to show you how well I could provide for a family."

This certainly was a problem. The father realized that even if he thought it was good for his daughter to marry a ghost, it was unlikely that she would consent to marry one. The father thought quickly, trying to find a way to get his family out of this predicament without angering a large, strong, monstrous ghost who could easily kill them all if he decided to.

"Yes," said the father, "you have certainly shown that you will be an excellent provider, and I'm sure you'll make someone a fine husband someday. But there is a tradition among my people, a sort of challenge that suitors must conquer before he can marry one of our daughters."

"Oh?" said the ghost. "What challenge is that?"

"It's a little game called hide-the-plum-pit. We have to play it in order to see whether you are worthy to marry my daughter. If you win, you can marry her. If I win, you need to give something to our family."

"Hmm," said the ghost. "I have never heard of such a challenge or such a tradition. Are you sure we have to do this?"

"Oh, yes," said the father. "We must. This has always been the way of our people, and if we don't play the game first, then our family will be cursed."

"I would never want to be the cause of anyone being cursed," said the ghost. "I agree to your terms. What is it you would like me to give to your family if I lose?"

"Please continue bringing us fresh meat. You're such a good hunter, and we have been so grateful for your help."

"Very well," said the ghost. "Let's play the game."

The father brought out the plum pit, and they began to play the game. Now, the father had suggested this challenge because he knew no one could ever beat him at this game, even if it were a ghost from the land of the dead. The father's hands moved so fast that the ghost couldn't possibly find the plum pit, no matter how hard or how many times he tried. And of course it didn't help that the daughter had taken out her drum and had begun to play it and sing songs, which distracted the ghost no end.

Finally, the ghost gave up. "You win. I can't possibly defeat you. I'm very sorry that I won't be able to marry your daughter, but I will keep my end of the bargain."

"You are very gracious," said the father. "I hope you do find someone to marry soon."

And so the ghost continued bringing the family meat for the rest of their lives, but no one knows whether he ever found himself a wife.

The First Fog *(Inuit, Arctic)*

Sometimes creative acts happen out of the destruction of something evil, as in this Inuit story of how fog came into the world. A bad spirit has been graverobbing and then eating the bodies, and does not stop until the village angakkuq *deals with him. An* angakkuq *is a person who holds a special place in Inuit culture as a spiritual leader, peacekeeper, and shaman. This role may be filled by either men or women, but it is more common for men to become an* angakkuq.

In this story, we see the importance of the angakkuq *to the safety of his people and his role as someone able to deal with supernatural threats. When the people are troubled by the disturbance of their loved ones' graves by a bad spirit, it is the* angakkuq *who puts himself in jeopardy in order to discover why the graverobbing has been happening and to dispatch any supernatural beings who might be responsible. The* angakkuq *in this story also functions as a trickster, deceiving the bad spirit's wife about how to cross the river created by the* angakkuq's *magic, which results in the creation of the first fog.*

A long time ago, the people had a very dire problem. A bad spirit was coming down out of the mountains and stealing the bodies of the dead from their graves. No one knew who the spirit was or where it lived, and it was frightening to think that the spirit could come and steal a loved one's body any time it wished.

Finally the village *angakkuq* had had enough. He asked his fellow villagers to have a funeral and bury him as though he were dead. "I will wait in the grave for this spirit to come and get me," said the *angakkuq*, "and when it does, I will find out how to make it leave our loved ones' bodies in peace."

At first, the villagers were hesitant. "What if you die for real before the spirit comes to get you? What if the spirit kills you and eats you? What will we do then, if you are no longer here to help us?"

But the *angakkuq* reassured all the villagers that this was the best way to stop the spirit, and so they had a funeral for him and buried him in a grave as though he were dead. That night, after all the people had gone to their homes, the spirit came down out of the mountains to see whether any new bodies had been buried that day. He looked in the graveyard and saw the place where the *angakkuq* had just been buried. The spirit dug up the *angakkuq* and slung his body over his shoulders. Then he walked all the long way back to his house in the mountains.

When the spirit got home, he put the *angakkuq* down and said to his wife, "This one was heavier than all the others. I am very tired. I am going to sleep for a while."

"Very well," said the spirit's wife. "I will go out and gather firewood so that we can cook and eat this one later."

After the spirit's wife had gone, the *angakkuq* opened his eyes. The spirit's children had been watching him and saw him do this.

"Father! Father! This one isn't dead!" they cried.

"Hush," said the spirit. "I dug him out of the grave just this very night. He's dead for sure. Now let me sleep."

When the spirit rolled over to go back to sleep, the *angakkuq* jumped up and killed both the spirit and the spirit's children with his knife.

Then the *angakkuq* ran out of the spirit's house and down the path that would take him back to his own village. As he ran, the *angakkuq* passed the spirit's wife as she was returning home with a load of firewood. At first, the spirit's wife thought that the *angakkuq* was her husband. "Where are you going in such a hurry?" she said as the *angakkuq* sped past.

Still thinking she had seen her husband running, and wondering what he was up to, the spirit's wife ran after the *angakkuq*. The *angakkuq* heard the footsteps of the spirit's wife following him. Soon the *angakkuq* reached a stream. He leapt over it easily. Then he turned and said to the stream, "Swell with water, little stream! Overflow your banks!"

By the time the spirit's wife arrived, the stream had turned into a wide river. It was so wide, the spirit's wife could not jump across it. She saw the *angakkuq* on the other side and shouted, "How did you get across this river?"

"Oh, it was very easy," said the *angakkuq*. "I just drank up all the water until the streambed was dry."

The spirit's wife knelt on the bank and began to drink. She drank and drank and drank until the streambed was completely dry. Then she started walking across. When she was in the middle of the streambed, the *angakkuq* said, "What is that dangling down from your private parts? Do spirits like you have tails like beasts do?"

The spirit's wife stopped and bent over to look. But because she was so full of water, her belly burst open when she bent over, and she died. The water that came out of her belly turned into fog, and this was the very first fog that ever existed. From then on, the people could bury their dead in peace, and no one disturbed the graves.

Coyote and the Origin of Death *(Caddo, Southeast))*

Coyote is a common figure in Indigenous myths, where he functions variously as a trickster, gullible mark, creator, or some mixture thereof. In this myth from the Caddo people of the southeastern

United States, Coyote is responsible for death becoming permanent. However, he does this not through spite or by mistake but rather out of concern for the living, since if people do not die, there soon will be too many people, leading to a dearth of resources and much suffering. Despite Coyote's good intentions, the fact that he is the one who makes death a permanent state marks him as a pariah ever after.

In the beginning of the world, people never died. They just went on living and having children, and soon the world became too crowded and there was not enough food to go around. All the chiefs got together to hold a council to decide what to do.

One chief stood up and said, "I think we should have people die, but only for a little while. After they have been dead for a time, let them come back."

When that chief was done speaking, Coyote stood up and said, "Oh, no. That is a terrible plan. If people come back after a little while, we will still have the same problem because no one will ever go away forever. I think death should be something that is for always."

The other chiefs were dismayed by Coyote's words. "We should let people come back!" cried one.

"Yes!" cried another. "It's not fair that they should go away forever. Their families and friends will miss them so much if they know the dead will never return."

Many other chiefs also stood and spoke against Coyote's plan, and in the end, the council decided that people should die for a little while and then come back to life again. The medicine men then went about building a grass house facing to the east. This was a special house in which the dead were to be brought back to life.

"We will put an eagle feather over the door," said the chief medicine man, "and when somebody dies, the feather will fall off the door and turn red with blood. Then all the medicine men will know to come to the grass house and sing the spirit of the dead person back to life."

When the people heard the new rules about death, they agreed that this was a good plan. They did not want their friends and family members to be gone forever.

After a time, the feather over the grass house grew red with blood and fell off the door. The medicine men all went into the grass house, and for about ten days they sang to bring the spirit back to life. When they were done singing, the young man who had died was standing there in the middle of the grass house, alive again. Everyone who had known the young man rejoiced that he was alive among them once more.

Coyote saw what the medicine men had done. He saw the young man brought back to life and how the people rejoiced to see him again. But Coyote was not pleased. He wanted death to be forever because otherwise there wouldn't be enough food for everyone.

The next time the feather fell from the door, Coyote went into the grass house with the medicine men. Coyote sat there while they sang to bring the spirit back. After they had sung for many days, Coyote heard the sound of a whirlwind approaching the grass house. He heard the wind start to whirl and whirl around the house as the medicine men sang. Coyote knew that the spirit of the dead person was in this wind, and so when the wind approached the door of the house and tried to enter, Coyote jumped up and slammed the door shut, keeping the spirit outside. When the spirit saw that the door of the grass house was shut, it moved on with the whirlwind and never came back.

Because Coyote closed the door to the grass house that way, the spirits of the dead are never able to return to the land of the living. And when the people hear and see a whirlwind, they say, "Oh, that must be the spirit of someone who has just died. They are wandering and looking for a way to go to the land of the spirits."

Coyote, for his part, was frightened by what he had done, and so he ran away. And ever since that time, he has been very cautious because he always fears that he will be punished for making death last forever, and he is always very hungry for no one will give him food anymore.

Blue Jay and the Ghosts *(Chinook, Northwest Coast)*

Blue Jay is a trickster figure in the mythology of the Chinook people of the Pacific Northwest. Like many tricksters, Blue Jay is vain and selfish, and he likes to purposely go against the advice of others, especially that of his sister, Io'i. Blue Jay dismisses his sister's wisdom very frequently, often with the untrue observation that "Io'i always tells lies."

This story, which is primarily set in the world of the afterlife, both explains how ghosts continue their existence in the ghost world and also describes what that world is like, both for the ghosts who live there and for the living who might chance to visit them. The importance of politeness and respect, even to the ghosts of the dead, is a primary theme of this story, as is the importance of following directions given by a knowledgeable person, things that Blue Jay learns the hard way and at permanent cost to himself.

There was a time when some ghosts decided they needed a woman to be a wife for their chief. They looked among the living for the woman who would best suit. When they found her, they went to her family bearing a great wealth of dentalia shells, and her family agreed to the marriage. Io'i was married to the ghosts that night, but when everyone rose in the morning, they found that she had disappeared. Io'i's brother, Blue Jay, said, "I'll wait for a year, and if she has not reappeared or sent us a message, I'll go and look for her."

A year passed with no word from Io'i, so Blue Jay set out to find her. First he went and asked all the trees, "Where do people go when they die?" But the trees didn't answer him, so then Blue Jay asked all the birds. They didn't answer him either. Finally, Blue Jay asked an old wedge that belonged to him. "I know where people go when they die," said the wedge, "but I won't take you there unless you pay me." Blue Jay paid the wedge, and it took him to the land of the ghosts.

In the land of the ghosts, there was a large village with many houses. Blue Jay walked through the village, noticing that none of the houses had smoke rising from them, except for one very large house at the other end. Blue Jay went to the large house and entered. Inside he found his sister. They were very happy to see one another again, and after they had exchanged greetings, Io'i asked, "Why are you here? Are you dead now?"

"No, I'm not dead at all," said Blue Jay. "I paid my old wedge to carry me here."

Then Blue Jay went out of the big house and wandered through the village. He looked into each and every house, and found that all of them were full of bones. He returned to the big house, where he saw a pile of bones near where his sister was sitting.

"Why are all these bones in your house?" said Blue Jay.

Io'i pointed to one skull and said, "That's your brother-in-law."

Blue Jay thought, "That can't possibly be my brother-in-law. Io'i lies all the time."

But after sunset, when it was dark, the bones turned into the shapes of people, who began to go about their business. Blue Jay looked at them closely, but he found it difficult to see their features and their clothing.

"Where did all these people come from?" Blue Jay asked Io'i. "Where did all the bones go?"

"Don't be silly," said Io'i. "These aren't people. They're ghosts."

Blue Jay thought this a little frightening, but he said, "That's all right. I'd like to stay with you all the same."

"Very well," said Io'i. "How about going fishing? You can take your dip net and go out with that boy over there. He is a relative of my husband. But don't talk to him while you're out fishing together."

Blue Jay was unsure how he would talk to the boy, even assuming he found something to say. The ghosts only whispered, and no matter how hard Blue Jay tried, he couldn't understand what they said.

The ghost boy and Blue Jay went down to the river and launched their canoe, the ghost boy in the stern and Blue Jay in the bow. They paddled along for a while, and soon they came across a large group that was also paddling down the river. All the other people were singing as they paddled. Blue Jay recognized the song and joined in, but as soon as he started singing loudly, everyone else stopped. Blue Jay turned around to look at the ghost boy but saw that he had turned into a pile of bones.

For a while, Blue Jay continued to paddle along the river, neither speaking nor singing. Then he decided to turn around and see what had become of the ghost boy. When he looked, he saw that the bones had disappeared, and the ghost boy was sitting in the stern just as he had done when they started out.

Speaking very softly, Blue Jay asked the boy, "How far is it to your weir?"

"A little farther down the river," said the boy.

They paddled on for a short time. Then in a very loud voice Blue Jay asked, "How far is it to your weir?" When Blue Jay turned around, he found that the boy had turned into a pile of bones again.

Blue Jay remained silent for a few moments, then turned around and saw the boy sitting there. Blue Jay asked very softly, "How far is it to your weir?"

"It's right here," said the boy.

Blue Jay took his dip net and started to fish with it. He put the net in the water and brought up two branches, which he threw back in.

Again Blue Jay dipped his net, this time bringing up a load of wet leaves. Blue Jay threw these back, too, but some of them landed in the bottom of the canoe, where the boy scooped them up.

They fished for a little longer, but all Blue Jay managed to catch were two more branches. "Oh, well," thought Blue Jay, "we may not be able to eat these, but they're still useful. I'll give them to Io'i to use on the fire."

The boy and Blue Jay paddled back home. It was very frustrating to Blue Jay to return with only two branches to show for all their work, but when they beached the canoe and headed back to the big house, Blue Jay noticed the boy carrying a mat full of trout. "That's odd," thought Blue Jay. "He never caught anything the whole time we were fishing."

The boy gave the fish to his people to cook. "Why do you have so few fish?" they asked.

"Blue Jay threw out almost everything he caught," said the boy. "It was so wasteful. He caught many fine, large fish, but then he just tossed them back into the water."

Io'i asked Blue Jay, "Why did you throw all the fish away?

"Fish?" said Blue Jay. "I didn't catch a single one. All I caught were a bunch of branches and a net full of leaves."

"Well, exactly," said Io'i. "You threw away a lot of good fish. The leaves were trout, and the branches were salmon."

Io'i left the house and went down to the riverbank. She looked inside the boy's canoe, and inside she found two very large salmon. She picked them up and brought them back to the house.

When Blue Jay saw his sister carrying the salmon, he was very surprised. "Where on earth did you get those?" he asked. "Did you steal them from somewhere?"

"Don't be silly," said Io'i. "You caught these. They were in your canoe."

But Blue Jay didn't believe his sister. "Io'i always lies," he thought to himself.

In the morning, Blue Jay went down to the riverside. He looked at all the canoes that had been beached there. Blue Jay wondered how he and the boy had been able to paddle out and not sink, since every single one of the canoes had holes in it, and in places they were dotted with moss and lichens.

Blue Jay returned to the house. "Your husband doesn't take very good care of his canoes," he said.

"Please stop complaining," said Io'i. "You're going to offend my husband and his family."

"But all the canoes are full of holes and have moss growing on them!"

"Well, of course they do!" said Io'i. "Don't you understand? These aren't living people here. They're all dead. They're all ghosts. They don't do things the same way you do in the land of the living."

After sunset, Blue Jay and the ghost boy went fishing again. This time Blue Jay teased the boy by shouting at him to turn him into bones, then being quiet until he became a boy again. Soon they arrived at the weir and began to fish. Every time Blue Jay caught some leaves or branches, he put them in the bottom of the canoe instead of throwing them away. When the canoe was full, they paddled back, and on the way home Blue Jay teased every ghost they met by shouting at them and turning them into bones. The boy and Blue Jay arrived back at the village. They beached their canoe and brought their catch into the big house.

"Look what we caught today!" Blue Jay announced as he gave his sister a great pile of big, fat salmon.

The next evening, Blue Jay went for a walk through the ghost village. When it was fully dark, all the bones turned into people and began to go about their business. As he walked, Blue Jay heard someone call out, "Look! There's a whale on the beach!"

Blue Jay headed back to the big house to find out more. His sister met him on his way. She pressed a knife into his hands and said, "Go and help carve up that whale!"

But Blue Jay didn't know exactly where the whale was. He went to the first ghost he saw and said very loudly, "Where is the whale?" but the ghost couldn't answer because it had turned all to bones. Frustrated, Blue Jay kicked the skull.

Blue Jay went on his way, asking every ghost about the whale, but he kept asking in a loud voice, and the ghosts kept turning into bones. Finally Blue Jay came across a large tree trunk at the edge of the river. The tree trunk had very thick bark, which the ghost people were stripping off with their knives. Blue Jay shouted at them, and the people all turned to bones. Then Blue Jay went up to the tree trunk and began peeling off some of the bark. He found that it was full of pitch. When he had peeled two big pieces, he picked them up and brought them home.

Blue Jay dumped the bark pieces just outside the house, then brought his sister out to show her. "Look at this!" said Blue Jay. "Everyone kept saying it was a whale, but it's nothing but a big tree with thick bark!"

"What are you talking about?" said Io'i. "That's whale meat right there. And it's good whale meat, too. Look at all the blubber!"

Blue Jay looked down, and sure enough, instead of two big pieces of bark, there were two big pieces of whale meat. When he looked up, Blue Jay saw another ghost coming toward the big house carrying a big piece of tree bark. Blue Jay shouted at the ghost, and it collapsed into a heap of bones. Blue Jay picked up the piece of tree bark and brought it back to the house. Then he went back out and did this over and over again, collecting all the whale meat that the ghosts were bringing home.

In the morning, Blue Jay thought that he would have some fun with the skeletons in the village. He went into a house where there were bones from a child and an adult. He picked up the skulls and put the child's skull on the adult's skeleton. Then he put the adult skull on the child's skeleton. Going from house to house, he switched up all the skulls that were there. When it got dark, the ghosts were in terrible distress! No one had the correct head. The children could not sit up properly because their heads were too big for their bodies. The adults all felt strange because their heads were too small for their bodies.

The next morning, Blue Jay put the skulls back on the proper bodies. Then he decided to play the same kind of trick, except with the legs. He gave the children's legs to the adults, and the adults' legs to the children. If there weren't enough children's bones, he'd swap a man's legs for a woman's, or the other way around.

Blue Jay thought himself a very clever fellow, but the ghosts soon became tired of all of his tricks. Io'i's husband said to her, "It's time your brother went home. He's behaving very rudely, and the people don't like him at all."

Io'i asked Blue Jay to stop behaving so badly, but he wouldn't listen. He kept doing things to the ghost people's skeletons in the daytime, and teasing them by shouting at them and turning them back into bones at night.

One day, Blue Jay went into the big house, where he found his sister cradling the skull of her husband. Blue Jay snatched it out of her hands and tossed it away. "Oh, no!" cried Io'i. "You have broken your brother-in-law's neck!"

When night fell, Io'i's husband was gravely ill. A shaman came to the big house and was able to heal him.

At last Blue Jay decided he should go home. Io'i handed him five buckets of water. "Now, listen carefully!" she said. "You will have to pass through five prairies and five woodlands on your way home. The prairies will all be on fire, but you must save all your water until you get to the fourth prairie. Don't forget what I just told you."

"I won't," said Blue Jay.

Blue Jay headed out with his five buckets of water. He walked until he came to a prairie. It was very hot there, and the prairie was dotted with red flowers. "This is probably what Io'i meant," said Blue Jay, and he poured out half of his first bucket onto the prairie, dripping the water onto the trail as he walked along.

Then Blue Jay walked on, and at the end of that first prairie he came to a woodland. He walked through the woodland and came to a second prairie. This one was on fire at the edge. He poured out the second half of his bucket onto that fire, and half of the next bucket as well. When he reached the end of the second prairie, he came to another woodland, and having crossed that, he came to the third prairie. Instead of just being hot or just being on fire on the edge, half of this prairie was ablaze. He poured one and a half buckets onto that fire and reached the woodland on the other side in safety.

Blue Jay came to a fourth prairie. This time, almost the whole thing was on fire, and Blue Jay only had two and a half buckets of water left. He poured out the half bucket that was left and then another half from one of the full buckets, and reached the woodlands in safety.

Finally Blue Jay came to the fifth prairie. This one was entirely on fire, and Blue Jay had only one bucket of water left. He poured out the whole thing as he walked along, and when he got to the end of his water he still had a little way to go to get to the woodland. Blue Jay took his bearskin blanket and tried to use it to beat out the flames, but the blanket caught fire and burned right up. Then the fire began to burn Blue Jay's hair, and soon he was dead, having been burnt to death by the prairie fire.

Around sunset, Blue Jay headed back to his sister's house. When he arrived on the bank of the river opposite from where she lived, he called out to her. Io'i came to the river and saw her brother's ghost standing on the other side.

"Oh, no!" cried Io'i. "My brother is truly dead."

Io'i took her husband's canoe and paddled it across to get her brother. When she arrived, Blue Jay said, "Where did you get this beautiful canoe? I've never seen one better."

"This is my husband's canoe, the one you said was all full of holes and covered in moss."

Blue Jay said, "Io'i, you always lie. Maybe this is your husband's canoe, but I know the other ones were all full of holes and had moss all over them."

"Blue Jay, you're dead now," said Io'i. "Things will look different to you here because now you're a ghost."

Soon they arrived at the village of the ghosts. Blue Jay and Io'i beached the canoe and headed back to the big house. Blue Jay saw all the ghosts going about their business. Some of them were playing games. Others were singing. Still others were dancing. Blue Jay tried to join in the singing, but all the ghosts laughed at him.

Io'i brought her brother into the big house. There Blue Jay saw a very handsome man, who obviously was a chief.

"Who is that?" said Blue Jay to his sister.

"Don't be silly," said Io'i. "That's my husband, your brother-in-law. You broke his neck once, remember?"

"And all those canoes on the riverbank," said Blue Jay, "they were just as beautiful as the one belonging to your husband. Not one of them had any holes or even one speck of moss."

"Oh, Blue Jay," said Io'i, "don't you understand? You're dead now, so you see the land of the ghosts the same way they do."

But Blue Jay didn't want to believe his sister. "Io'i lies all the time," he thought to himself.

Blue Jay decided to try one of his old tricks. He went up to a group of people and shouted at them, but instead of turning into piles of bones, they just laughed at him. When Blue Jay saw this trick wasn't working, he stopped trying.

Later, Blue Jay went for a walk again and found a group of magicians who were singing and dancing.

"Please share your powers with me!" said Blue Jay, but the magicians only laughed at him.

After a little while, Io'i came looking for her brother and found him watching the magicians and asking them for their powers.

"Don't be silly," Io'i said to Blue Jay. "Come home, and leave these people alone."

Blue Jay went home with his sister, but the next night he went back to the place where the magicians did their dancing. Again he asked them to share their powers with him, and again the magicians just laughed at him. Night after night, Blue Jay went to the magicians and asked for their powers, and on the fifth night the magicians had had enough. They sent Blue Jay walking back to the big house on his hands, his legs waving in the air.

Io'i saw her brother prancing about on his hands. She began to weep and mourn. "Oh, Blue Jay," she cried, "now I have seen you die a second time, for the magicians have taken your wits from you."

Part III: Trickster Tales

Coyote and Little Turtle *(Hopi, Southwest)*

This story from the Hopi people of Arizona shows Coyote in his guise as a gullible creature who can be tricked into just about anything. When Coyote tries to bully a small turtle into singing for him, the turtle makes Coyote's gullible nature work to his own advantage, tricking Coyote into throwing him into the water, which is just where the turtle wants to be.

Near the village of Orayvi, there is a spring called Leenangva. All around the spring grew rushes and cattails and other plants that liked the water, and among the plants lived a family of turtles. The turtles lived there very happily. They had plenty of water and plenty of food to eat.

But there came a time when the rain did not fall. After a while, the streams and ponds began to dry up, and soon Leenangva also became dry. All the plants withered and died. It was hard for the animals who lived near the spring to find food.

Mother Turtle gathered up all her children and said, "We can't stay here. There is not enough water. There is not enough food. We need to go someplace else. We will go back to Sakwavayu, the Blue Lake, where we used to live. Maybe there is enough food and water there."

And so the turtles began to walk to Sakwavayu, where they used to live. Because it was so very dry, and because the day was so very bright, the sand was extremely hot. The smallest turtle had a hard time walking because the hot sand burned his feet. He became very tired and footsore, so he stopped to rest in the shade of a bush, thinking that he'd sit there until he had cooled off and then go follow his mother and brothers and sisters. It was nice and cool in the shade, and Little Turtle was so very, very tired. Soon he fell asleep. Mother Turtle did not even notice that he was missing. None of the other small turtles noticed that he was missing either.

Sometime later, Little Turtle woke up. "Oh, dear, oh dear!" he cried. "I fell asleep for I don't know how long, and now Mother Turtle and my brothers and sisters have gone on without me!"

Little Turtle began to weep because he was lonely and frightened. He came out from under the bush and saw the tracks his family had left, going in the direction of Ismo'wala. Little Turtle started following the tracks, weeping bitter tears the whole time, fearing that he would never see his family again. And still the sand was so very hot and hurt his feet so very much.

Now, Coyote lived in Ismo'wala, and he heard the sound of Little Turtle crying. He went to see who was making that sound, and found Little Turtle weeping and following the tracks his family had made. Little Turtle saw Coyote coming, so he flopped down on his stomach and pulled his head and all his legs into his shell. Coyote went up to Little Turtle and sniffed and snuffed around him. Then he took his paw and flipped Little Turtle over onto his back.

"Sing me that song you were singing," demanded Coyote.

"I wasn't singing. I was crying," said Little Turtle.

"A likely story," said Coyote. "Sing me that song."

"I already told you. I wasn't singing, I was crying," said Little Turtle. "I fell asleep under that bush, and my family went on without me. I was crying because I'm afraid I'll never see them again."

"Oh, come on and sing already," said Coyote. "We both know you were really singing. If you don't sing, I'll gobble you right up!"

"You go ahead and do that," said Little Turtle. "It wouldn't kill me anyway. I'd still be alive inside your belly."

"Well, then, if you won't sing, I'll take you up that mountain over there and push you down the side," said Coyote. "You'll slide and slide on the snow."

"That's all right with me," said Little Turtle. "Sliding on the snow sounds like fun!"

"Well, then, if you won't sing, I'll take you and roll you around and around in the sand here," said Coyote. "It's very hot, and I bet you won't like that at all."

"Hot sand doesn't bother me," said Little Turtle, "and rolling around in it sounds like fun."

Coyote began to feel frustrated. Nothing he could threaten Little Turtle with scared him at all. Then Coyote had an idea.

"If you won't sing me your song," said Coyote, "I'll take you down to the river and throw you right in!"

"Oh, no!" cried Little Turtle. "Please don't do that. Please do anything else you like to me, but don't throw me in the river!"

"Hah!" said Coyote. Then he picked up Little Turtle in his jaws and trotted down to the riverbank. The river had plenty of water in it, and it was running fast. Coyote threw Little Turtle into the water. As soon as he was in the river, Little Turtle stuck his head and legs out. He called to Coyote and said, "Thank you so much! The river is where I live. Thank you for throwing me in!"

Coyote could not believe his ears. He became very angry. "I will eat that Little Turtle if it's the last thing I do!" he said, and then he jumped into the water. Little Turtle saw him coming, and dove under the surface. Coyote tried to catch Little Turtle, but the river was so full and moving so fast that Coyote drowned.

When Little Turtle saw that Coyote couldn't follow him anymore, he came to the surface and began to swim along. He knew the river would take him to Sakwavayu. Little Turtle soon reached Sakwavayu, where he saw that his family had not yet arrived, so he crept under a bush to wait for them. Little Turtle waited and waited, until the sun had nearly set and the sand had cooled. Then he heard the sounds of his mother and brothers and sisters talking and laughing as they walked along. Little Turtle came out from under the bush and shouted "Surprise!" at his family.

"My goodness!" said Mother Turtle. "How did you get here so fast?"

"When we were walking, I stopped to rest under a bush. I fell asleep. When I woke up, I saw that you had gone on without me. I was crying because I was afraid I'd never see you again. I started following your tracks, but Coyote heard me crying. He thought I was singing. He said that if I didn't sing for him, he'd eat me. Then he said he'd make me slide down the mountain on the snow. Then he said he'd roll me around in the hot sand. When he said all those things, I told him I wasn't afraid. Then he said he'd throw me in the river. I pretended to be very afraid, so he picked me up in his jaws and threw me in the water. I thanked him for bringing me to my home, but this made him angry. He jumped into the river, saying he was going to eat me, but the water was too deep and too fast for him, and he drowned. When I knew it was safe, I swam along the river until I arrived here, where I waited for you."

"What a good thing that silly Coyote believes anything anyone tells him!" said Mother Turtle. "I am very glad you were able to trick him like that. Now, let's go down to the water and find something to eat."

The turtle family went down to the water, where they found many good things to eat. And they lived at Sakwavayu ever after.

Coyote and Fox *(Shuswap, Subarctic)*

If the Coyote of the Hopi story is impatient and gullible, the Coyote of this Shuswap story is vain and vengeful, although here he certainly has good reason to be angry at first. We also see an example of the way that animal characters in Indigenous tales are seen as people, doing human things like hunting with weapons, using fire, and making and wearing clothing.

This story functions both as a cautionary tale and as a just-so story. It is a cautionary tale in that it shows us the price paid by people who are vain and greedy, and a just-so story that explains why the fur of the silver fox is considered to be so valuable. However, it is only the vengeful Coyote who pays a price for his sins; Fox steals Coyote's food and is just as vain of his fine cloak as Coyote initially is of his, but Fox gets away with a full stomach and his fine cloak intact.

Coyote was always traveling about, and one time he became hungry as he walked along. He came upon a dwelling inhabited by rock rabbits. Coyote thought to himself, "Now those would make a tasty meal, for sure!" So Coyote killed all the rock rabbits and strung them together on a string. He put the string over his shoulder and went on his way, thinking that he'd travel for a bit longer before eating his catch.

The day was very clear and very hot. Soon Coyote was tired and so hungry he couldn't go any farther. He found a good shady pine tree and sat beneath it. To cook his rock rabbits, Coyote first made a big fire. When it was nice and hot, he put large stones in the fire. While the stones were heating, Coyote dug a hole, and when the stones were hot enough, Coyote put the stones in the hole. Coyote put the rock rabbits on top of the hot stones and covered them well with leaves and the dirt he dug out of the hole. Then he lay down in the shade of the tree to take a nap while his meal was cooking.

Now, Fox was also out and about on his travels, and as he walked along he saw Coyote asleep in the shade of the tree. Fox also saw the earth oven that Coyote was using to cook his meal. "I wonder what is cooking in there?" thought Fox, because he had been traveling all day and was very hungry. "I'll just go and have a little peek. Coyote's asleep; he won't even notice me."

Fox went over to the oven and dug out the rock rabbits, which were perfectly cooked. Fox gulped down half of them and was about to take the next one when Coyote said, "I don't mind sharing; just leave ten of them for me." Coyote didn't even sit up or open his eyes, he was that lazy.

Fox ate even more of the rock rabbits. "Leave nine of them for me, will you?" said Coyote.

But Fox kept on eating and eating, even though Coyote kept asking him to leave some for his own meal. Soon there was only one rock rabbit left. "Oh, well," said Coyote, "how about you leave half of that one for me?"

Fox didn't listen. He swallowed every last bite, and then all the rock rabbits were gone. Fox knew that Coyote would be very angry with him, so he left as fast as he could. This wasn't very fast, though, because Fox was so stuffed with good rock rabbits that he couldn't move very well, and soon he could go no farther. He lay down in the shade of a tree and went to sleep.

When Coyote realized that Fox had left after eating all the rock rabbits, he was furious. "That Fox! He didn't even leave one morsel for me! I'll show him!"

Coyote followed Fox's trail. Soon he came upon the place where Fox was fast asleep under the thick boughs of the tree. Using his magic, Coyote made the tree fall over on top of Fox. "There!" said Coyote. "That'll teach him to steal all my food!"

But the branches of the tree were so thick that the trunk never touched Fox at all. Fox squirmed his way through the thick branches and scurried away. Coyote saw him leaving and followed after, angrier than ever. Soon Fox came to a thick meadow of rye grass. He went deep into the grass, curled up, and went to sleep. Coyote watched Fox go into the grass, and when he was sure Fox was asleep, he set fire to the meadow. Fox woke up when he heard the sound of the approaching flames. He set his own back fire, and so he was able to escape.

Fox went to a place that was thickly grown with reeds. He went into the reeds thinking that maybe he'd finally be able to finish his sleep. But when he entered the reedy place, a great many hares jumped up and started running away. Coyote was still on Fox's trail, and so he saw all the hares running away. "Oh, this is fortunate!" said Coyote. "Now I'll be able to have a meal at last!"

Coyote set about killing the hares. Fox peered out from among the reeds and saw that Coyote was busy, so Fox slunk away. Coyote caught sight of Fox when he was a good way away, but now that Coyote had a great many fat hares to eat, he was content. "Fine, you can leave," Coyote called to Fox.

Coyote continued his travels until he came to a place where there were a great many magpies. Coyote set snares for the birds. When he had caught enough birds, he skinned them and made himself a fine cloak out of the skins with the feathers still attached. "Why, look how handsome this cloak is!" Coyote said. "No one will look better than me." Then Coyote made a song about how beautiful his cloak was and how pleased he was with it.

Again Coyote resumed his journey. Soon he crossed paths with Fox again. This time, Fox was wearing his own fine cloak, but this one was made of silver fox skins and was adorned with golden eagle feathers. Coyote was instantly envious of Fox's cloak, so he said, "Hey, Fox! Would you like to trade cloaks with me?"

"Of course not!" said Fox. "Why would I trade a cloak of fox fur and eagle feathers for one that is only made from magpie skins?"

Coyote pretended to accept Fox's answer. He turned away as though he were going to leave, but then suddenly jumped at Fox and snatched away the fur cloak.

Coyote ran and ran, clutching the fur cloak. Soon he came to a lake. He took the magpie-skin robe and tore it into pieces, then threw the pieces into the water. He picked up the fur cloak and put it on. My, how well he looked in it, and how beautiful the feathers were!

"I am the most beautiful creature on earth," said Coyote. "The only thing that is missing is a little breeze. How the feathers would flutter and dance if there was but a breath of wind! That is the only thing that would make me look better than I already do."

Now, Fox had followed after Coyote, and when Coyote got to the edge of the lake, Fox hid himself and waited to see what Coyote would do. When Fox heard Coyote wish for a breeze, Fox used his magic to call up a strong wind. The wind blew the fox-fur cloak off Coyote's back and carried it back to Fox.

Coyote knew he'd never get that fur cloak back, so he began to look around for the pieces of his magpie-skin cloak. But the wind had blown away many of the pieces, and the bits that Coyote was able to find had lost all their feathers.

Fox wore that cloak ever after, and soon he turned into an ordinary fox. This is why foxes have lovely silver fur, and why their fur is the most valuable one of all.

How Beaver Stole Fire *(Nez Perce, Plateau)*

A great many cultures have stories telling how one animal or another stole fire and gave it to the people. Coyote often plays this role, as does the opossum or, as in this story from the Nez Perce of the Columbia River Plateau in the Pacific Northwest, the beaver. Rather than being a substance that is simply created by or used by powerful beings, in this myth, fire is conceptualized as an inherent property of certain trees. The trees guard their fire jealously, and it's not until Beaver makes his brave attempt that fire is distributed to other trees and thus made available to other creatures as well.

Not only does this story explain how fire came to be used, but it also is a just-so story about certain geographical features. In Beaver's escape from the angry trees after stealing fire from them, the course that he runs along either digs or changes the channel of the Grande Ronde River.

In the time before there were any people in the world, animals and birds and plants walked and talked together just like people do now. And in that time, the only ones with the secret of fire were the pine trees. They guarded this secret very jealously and wouldn't give it to any of the other creatures, even if those creatures might freeze to death without it.

One winter, it was so very cold that all the animals were afraid they would freeze to death. Only the pine trees were warm, because they had fire. The animals held a council to see how they might go about stealing some of the pine trees' fire. They came up with plan after plan, but none of them ever succeeded until finally Beaver made an attempt.

Beaver knew that the pine trees were about to hold a great council near the banks of the Grande Ronde River in Idaho. He knew that it was so cold that the trees likely would light a fire to warm themselves. And so Beaver hid himself in a place where he could watch the pine trees as they prepared for their council. First, the trees went into the river to bathe, and the water was so very, very cold! Then the trees came out of the river, and they built a fire to warm themselves after having bathed. But even as they shivered while they warmed themselves, the trees were still very crafty; they posted guards to watch for any animals or birds that might try to steal their fire.

However, Beaver knew they would post guards, and so he hid himself in a good place before the guards were there, but after the fire had been lit. As Beaver expected, soon a live coal came rolling down from the trees' fire to the place where he was hiding. Beaver jumped out of his hiding place, grabbed the coal, and ran away as fast as he could. The trees saw Beaver running away with a piece of their fire, and they went after him in hot pursuit. Whenever the trees got too close, Beaver would dodge this way and that, and this is why the Grande Ronde River has places where it is straight and places where it is crooked and winding.

After a long chase, many of the trees got too tired to continue running after Beaver, so they planted themselves on the banks of the river where they were, making a forest so thick that even the best hunters had difficulty moving through it. A few of the trees kept running after Beaver, but eventually they got tired, too, and planted themselves where they stopped. This is why in some places along the river there is dense forest, while in other places there are only a few scattered trees.

One cedar tree stubbornly refused to give up the chase, and kept running after Beaver after nearly all the other trees had stopped and planted themselves. A handful of other trees came with the cedar. Finally the cedar realized that he would never catch Beaver. He looked about and saw a high hill not far off.

"I will go and climb that hill," said the cedar to the other trees who were with him, "and that way maybe we can see where Beaver goes, even if we can never catch him."

The other trees agreed this was a good plan, so the cedar climbed up to the top of the hill and planted himself there on the crown. He looked down and saw Beaver diving into Big Snake River at the place where the Grande Ronde empties into it. As the cedar watched, Beaver swam across the Big Snake. Then Beaver went to the willows that stood on the banks of the river and gave them some of the pine trees' fire. After that, Beaver ran along the banks of the river for a little way, then dove back in and gave some fire to the birches on the other side of the river. And this is why when people make fire, they use willow and birch wood, because they have the fire Beaver stole, fire that will come out of their wood when it is rubbed a certain way.

And the cedar who climbed the hill? He stands there still, all alone, looking out over the river and over the trees that got pieces of the pine trees' fire, and when people go by that place, they tell the story and point out the lone cedar who chased Beaver all the way to that very spot.

The Raven and the Marmot *(Alaska Native)*

Raven plays a similar role in Alaska Native folklore that Coyote does in the stories of more southerly cultures. Raven is a trickster and a creator, but his hubris often leads him to be tricked by other animals.

Here Raven's pride is hurt by insults thrown at him by a group of seabirds. He tries to patch up his wounded dignity by going after a marmot, but the marmot is a quick-thinking animal and soon devises a way to escape Raven's beak by flattering the bird about his dancing ability.

The connection between dance and ravens is important to many Alaskan and northern Pacific Coast peoples. Several tribes from those areas practice forms of the Raven Dance, wherein the dancers don large wooden raven masks and sometimes feathered capes representing the bird's wings.

Unfortunately, I was unable to determine which Alaskan culture produced this particular story, but in her collection of Alaskan folktales, author Katharine Judson says that it is from the Bering Strait.

It was a fine, sunny day, and Raven thought he might go see whether he could find anything to eat at the seashore. As he flew along over the beach, a group of seabirds saw him gliding past and began to make fun of him.

One seabird called out, "Look at that Raven! He thinks he's so great, but all he ever eats is dead things!"

"Yes," said another. "I think that's just disgusting."

Then the birds began to taunt Raven together. "Carrion-eater! Carrion-eater! All you eat is dead things, and your black feathers are ugly!"

Raven was very put out by what the seabirds said. He turned away from the sea and flew toward the mountains, muttering to himself all the way. When Raven arrived in the mountains, he landed, thinking to rest his wings but still fuming over the things the seabirds had said. Raven looked about him and saw a marmot hole in the ground. Raven went to see whether the marmot was at home, but before he could so much as stick his beak into the hole, a small voice behind him said, "Excuse me, but that's my home. I'd like to go in, please, but you're blocking the way."

Raven turned around, and there was the marmot, waiting patiently for Raven to move aside. "Why should I move?" said Raven. "In fact, I think that maybe I should just eat you right now. That'll show those nasty seabirds they're wrong."

Marmot was puzzled by Raven's reference to the seabirds, but he said nothing about it. Instead, he said, "Very well, you can eat me, but I was wondering whether you might do one very important thing for me first."

Raven always liked being told how important he was, so he said, "Tell me what that is, and I'll see."

"I've heard that you are the best dancer in the world. I think that I should very much like your dance to be the very last thing I ever see in this world. If I sing, will you dance?"

Raven was extremely flattered by this. "Certainly! Begin your song, and I will dance for you. You will die happy."

"Oh, thank you!" said Marmot, and then he began to sing:

> *Oh, Raven, how gracefully you dance!*
>
> *Oh, Raven, how beautiful your black feathers!*

How strong your black beak!

Oh, Raven, dance for me, dance for me!

While Marmot was singing, the Raven began to hop about, first on one leg, then on the other. To concentrate better on his gracefulness, Raven closed his eyes. Soon Raven had hopped away from Marmot's hole, and the little creature scurried down into his burrow as fast as he could. When Marmot was safe from Raven's beak, he faced the entrance to his burrow and laughed. "*Chik-kik-kik-kik-kik*! That was the most ridiculous thing I've ever seen! I almost couldn't sing because I was trying so hard not to laugh at you. And now you won't get to eat me, even though I am fat and juicy!"

Raven couldn't think of anything to say to Marmot, even though he was very, very angry, so he flew away.

Woodrat and Pine-nut-man *(Pomo, California)*

The Pomo people of California traditionally lived along the north-central coast of the state in what are now Mendocino and Sonoma Counties, with their territory extending as far inland as Clear Lake. Like other Indigenous groups, the Pomo have many trickster tales, some of which feature the ubiquitous Coyote. However, the Pomo also have stories involving a different trickster animal: Woodrat.

In this story, Woodrat tricks a strange manlike creature called Pine-nut-man, resulting in Pine-nut-man's eventual death from being drained of all the pine nuts that fill his skin. The villagers in the Sacramento Valley where Pine-nut-man meets his demise don't know what pine nuts are, but when they discover that they are good to eat, they greedily fight over them. This legend therefore functions as a just-so story, as many trickster tales do, showing both the cleverness of Woodrat and explaining the introduction of pine nuts into the Pomo diet as an important staple food.

The story below is based on one collected from Pomo informants by anthropologist Samuel Barrett in the early 20th century.

One day, Woodrat was feeling hungry, so he went out to gather pine nuts. When he got to the pine tree, he saw that Pine-nut-man had arrived there before him and was already up in the tree gathering pine cones. A few pine cones had fallen to the ground and lay at the foot of the tree. Woodrat picked up one of the pine cones and started digging out the seeds and eating them.

"Hey, brother-in-law!" Woodrat called to Pine-nut-man. "These are some awfully good pine nuts we have right here."

Pine-nut-man didn't pay any attention to Woodrat. He just went on picking pine cones and putting them into his carrying sack. Soon Pine-nut-man had picked all the cones on that tree. He climbed down with his sack and went a little way away from the tree, where he sat down and began to take the pine nuts out of their cones.

Woodrat watched Pine-nut-man for a while, and then he said, "I guess you don't want me here. Do you know what folks do when they don't want me around? They dig a big hole and throw me into it. I can't annoy people when I'm at the bottom of a hole."

Pine-nut-man was eager to get rid of Woodrat. He didn't like Woodrat watching him or talking to him while he was at his work. So, Pine-nut-man got his digging stick and began to dig a hole. He kept digging and digging until the hole was so deep, he could fit the whole length of his body into it standing up. Pine-nut-man had been digging for such a long time, he began to wonder whether Woodrat was even still there.

"Hey, Woodrat!" he called. "I'm almost done with the hole. Are you still there?"

"Oh, yes, I'm still here," said Woodrat, "but I'm not sure the hole is quite deep enough yet. Keep digging, and don't ask me any more questions."

While Pine-nut-man kept digging, Woodrat collected some rotten wood. Then he laid out his rabbit-skin blanket on the ground. He put the wood onto the blanket, and also a bow, some arrows, and a spear.

Then he wrapped all those things inside the blanket and tied it well with thongs. Woodrat spoke to the bundle. "Bundle," he said, "speak to Pine-nut-man as though you were me."

Then Woodrat put the bundle next to the lip of the hole and ran far away from that place. He ran and ran until he arrived in the Sacramento Valley. In the valley there was a sweat lodge, and Woodrat went inside.

While Woodrat was running away, Pine-nut-man was still digging the hole. Presently, the bundle said to him, "Hey, Pine-nut-man! The hole is deep enough. Come and throw me in. Surely I'll break my neck at the bottom, and I won't be able to bother you anymore."

Pine-nut-man climbed out of the hole. He picked up the rabbit-skin bundle, thinking that it was Woodrat. Then he threw the bundle down the hole. When the bundle struck the bottom, it burst open, and Pine-nut-man saw the wood and weapons that had been inside it.

"Well!" he said to himself. "That Woodrat is much cleverer than I gave him credit for. But I'm cleverer still. He may have fooled me once, but he'll never fool me again. I can even see through mountains, and I'm the best tracker in the world. I'll follow Woodrat's trail, and when I catch him, I'll pay him out for tricking me."

Pine-nut-man looked around, and soon he found Woodrat's trail. He began following it, running along the same track Woodrat had gone, toward the Sacramento Valley.

Back in the valley, Blue Jay was perched on top of the sweat lodge that Woodrat had gone inside. Blue Jay was the chief of the village, and he had made it his duty to look for enemies from time to time so that the villagers could protect themselves. In the distance, Blue Jay saw a man running toward the village very fast.

"Hey, Woodrat!" said Blue Jay. "There's a man running toward our village. He seems very angry. Would you happen to know who he is?"

"Oh, that would be Pine-nut-man," said Woodrat from inside the sweat lodge. "And yes, I expect he's quite angry. I played a very good trick on him earlier today. But I know how to deal with him. Make sure all the entrances to the sweat lodge are completely sealed up, except for one small hole right at the top. I'll take care of the rest."

The other creatures did as Woodrat said. They sealed up the sweat house very tightly and made a small hole at the very top.

Just as they finished that work, Pine-nut-man ran into the village. He saw the animals gathered near the sweat lodge and said, "I am looking for my brother-in-law. I love him very much and haven't seen him in a long time. Would you happen to know where he is?"

"I'm right here," said Woodrat. "I'm inside the sweat lodge."

Pine-nut-man walked all the way around the lodge, but since it had been completely sealed up, he saw no way in.

"How do I get in?" said Pine-nut-man.

"There's a little hole at the very top," said Woodrat. "That's the way in. That's how we do things here in this village."

Pine-nut-man climbed up to the top of the sweat lodge and began working his way into the small hole. It was a very tight fit, and he had to work very hard to move his body through the hole. When Pine-nut-man had managed to get the lower half of his body into the sweat lodge, Woodrat took a sharp stick and poked Pine-nut-man hard in the stomach. A trickle of pine nuts started coming out of the hole. Woodrat poked him again, and this time more pine nuts came out. Woodrat poked him over and over until a great stream of pine nuts came pouring out of Pine-nut-man's body and piling on the floor of the sweat lodge. Soon all that remained of Pine-nut-man was an empty skin with a head, hands, and feet attached to it. There wasn't even a skeleton, because Pine-nut-man's insides were made of nothing but pine nuts.

When what remained of Pine-nut-man fell all the way through the hole, Woodrat opened the sweat lodge, and the villagers came inside. The villagers picked up Pine-nut-man's remains and put them outside the lodge.

Blue Jay looked at the great mound of pine nuts that had fallen out of Pine-nut-man's body. "Whatever are these?" he asked. "I've never seen anything like them. Can we eat them? Has anyone ever seen these before?" But none of the villagers knew what the pine nuts were, so Blue Jay sent a messenger to the next village to see whether they had anyone who knew about pine nuts.

The messenger came back with Grey Squirrel. The villagers invited Grey Squirrel into the sweat lodge and offered him a seat. When Grey Squirrel was seated, Blue Jay said, "Welcome to our village. We asked you here because we need your help. We have this big mound of something here, and we don't know what it is. Maybe you can tell us whether these are good or not?"

"I've never seen those before either," said Grey Squirrel, "but I'll taste one and let you know whether they are good."

Grey Squirrel picked up a pine nut. He sniffed it, then nibbled a small bit off the end. His eyes grew very big. Then he ate the whole pine nut.

"Oh, yes, I do know what these are!" said Grey Squirrel. "My people eat them all the time. They're quite delicious; we think they're the best kind of food in the whole world!"

Then Grey Squirrel took the sack that he had brought with him and filled it with pine nuts to take home, but when the villagers realized that the pine nuts were good to eat, they each wanted to get as much for themselves as they could. They grabbed their own sacks and started stuffing them with pine nuts. Soon fights began to break out when some villagers thought that others had taken more than their fair share, and one person slashed at Grey Squirrel's sack so that all his pine nuts fell to the floor. Grey Squirrel didn't have another sack, and none of the villagers would lend him one of theirs, so he went home empty-handed.

Woodrat watched how the villagers behaved over the pine nuts. He became so disgusted that he left and went far away.

Part IV: Hero Tales

Manabozho Plays Lacrosse *(Menominee, Northeast Forest)*

Manabozho is a culture hero in Algonquin cultures in both the United States and Canada. He has many different powers, and functions as both a trickster and a creator, as many Indigenous culture heroes do. This story features the version of the hero held by the Menominee people of what is now northern Wisconsin.

The central event of this story is a big game of lacrosse organized by the sky spirits and the underground spirits. Each group of spirits puts together a team of creatures associated with their various realms and pits them in a cosmic match on a field that extends from Detroit to Chicago.

Played with a small ball and sticks having a net at one end, lacrosse is an Indigenous sport that has been played in the northern United States and in Canada for many centuries. Although modern regulation lacrosse is played by a relatively small number of players on a relatively small field, matches played by Indigenous peoples before the incursion of Europeans were between teams that could include hundreds of players on a field that was several miles long. For Indigenous peoples, lacrosse was and still is a sacred game and was an important expression both of tribal identity and of spiritual beliefs.

Manabozho was a very clever and powerful being. Some even say that he made the whole world. Manabozho had a son, whose name was Wolf. One winter's day, Wolf told his father that he was going out to hunt. Manabozho knew that Wolf liked to hunt in the estuary at Green Bay, which was frozen over at this time of year.

"Take care, my son," said Manabozho, "and stay off the ice at Green Bay. It is very dangerous."

Wolf went out to hunt. He followed the game all the way around the bay until he was on the opposite side from his home. Wolf was already tired from his long day of hunting, and the sun was beginning to set. Taking a shortcut across the ice was so very tempting! Wolf thought for a long moment about his father's warning, but then he decided to run across the ice. "I am the swiftest runner in the world," said Wolf. "Surely I'll be able to get to the other side without coming to any harm."

Wolf began to run across the ice. But when he was only about halfway across, the ice began to crack and shudder under him. It broke up into small pieces that whirled about in the current. The ice was very slippery, and Wolf could not keep his footing. He fell into the deep, freezing cold water, where he drowned.

When Manabozho found out that his son was dead, he grieved heavily. Day and night, he wept bitter tears for his son, and with each of his sobs, the earth shook. Even the spirits began to be afraid.

"Let's give him his son back," the underground spirits said. "Who knows what Manabozho might do if his son stays among the dead?"

And so it was that Wolf returned to his father. "Look, Father!" he said. "I am alive again!"

"It doesn't matter," said Manabozho. "I've already wept too much."

Manabozho took a long branch from the fire, its end still aflame, and gave it to Wolf. "Take this fire," said Manabozho, "and go into the west, as far as you can go. Light fires there. From now on, when people die, their spirits will go that way."

Even though the underground spirits had given Wolf back, Manabozho remained angry that his son had died, and he vowed to take revenge on the spirits for allowing that to happen. Manabozho waited and waited for the best opportunity, but for a long time nothing presented itself. Then one day Manabozho was walking along, and he heard someone whooping with joy. Manabozho went looking for whoever it was that was making the noise, and soon he came across a little fish called Nakuti, who had been whooping over and over again.

"Hey, Nakuti," said Manabozho, "what is going on that you are so happy? I heard you whooping from very far away."

"Oh, it's the very best thing," said Nakuti. "The great spirits above the sky have challenged the great spirits under the ground to a game of lacrosse, so we're all going to play lacrosse tomorrow! The fish and animals are going to play for the spirits below, and the birds and thunder-beings are going to play for the spirits above, and I can't wait!"

Manabozho thanked Nakuti for telling him about the game and then went his way, elated. This was it; this was the moment he had been waiting for. Manabozho would go to this lacrosse game, where all the spirits would be assembled, and there he would avenge his son's death.

The day before the lacrosse game, the underground spirits went looking for the best place from which to watch the game, one goal of which was in Detroit and the other in Chicago. The spirits came up out of the water and climbed up a mountain that overlooked the playing field. Satisfied that this was the best place, they went back to their homes. Manabozho saw their tracks going up the mountain and back down again. He climbed the mountain himself and realized what the underground spirits must have been doing. Manabozho turned himself into a pine tree that was all burnt on one side, and there on the mountaintop, he waited.

The next day at dawn, all the animals, fish, birds, and thunder-beings arrived at the playing field. Each team was making the most raucous noises they could, trying to frighten their opponents. When everyone had arrived, each creature took on a human form and took his place on the field. Once all the players were in place, they all fell silent until the ball was tossed into play. Then with a great roar from each side, the game began. Up and down the field they ran, each team fighting to get possession of the ball and hurl it through their opponent's goal.

At one point, one of the teams got the ball and surged toward the Chicago goal. The opposing team redoubled their efforts, and in the melee that ensued, everything was such a blur of lacrosse sticks, arms, legs, dust, and shouts that Manabozho could not see what was going on. In his excitement, he forgot that he was supposed to remain hidden as a tree, and turned himself back into a man, hoping that he would better be able to see the game.

The sudden appearance of Manabozho in their midst startled the underground spirits. Realizing that he had accidentally revealed himself, Manabozho took his bow and arrows and began shooting the spirits. The spirits scurried down the mountain and dove back into the lake, trying to evade Manabozho's arrows, but it was no use: whoever Manabozho aimed at was pierced by an arrow. The rush of so many spirits back into the waters caused great waves to form on the lake. The waves sped over the shore of the lake and onto the playing field.

Now, the lacrosse players had seen the underground spirits racing back to the lake, and had heard them shrieking "Manabozho! Manabozho!" as they fled. The players all returned to the center of the field to decide what was to be done. It was intolerable that someone would be so brash as to attack the underground spirits.

"How are we going to find and catch Manabozho?" said one player.

"We'll use the power of the water," said another.

"Yes! The water will be angry with him and will show us exactly where he has gone," said a third.

The other players agreed that this was a good plan, so they all waded into the lake. When everyone had entered the lake, the water rose up and rushed out of the lakebed, intent on catching Manabozho and punishing him for shooting at the underground spirits.

Manabozho, meanwhile, had stopped shooting at the spirits and had started running away, because he knew that the spirits and their allies would never let him go unpunished. He ran away from the lacrosse field as fast as he could, but soon he heard a rush of water behind him. He looked back and saw the waters of the lake flooding after him.

Manabozho was terrified. He redoubled his speed, but no matter how fast he ran, the waters still were catching up to him. Faster and faster Manabozho went, and closer and closer came the water. Finally Manabozho ran past a mountain. He changed course and ran up the mountainside, thinking that he'd be able to escape the water by climbing higher. But it was no use; the water climbed the sides of the mountain.

On the top of the mountain was a tall pine tree. Manabozho ran up to the tree and said, "Oh, Little Brother! The waters of the lake are chasing me and will drown me if they catch me. Can you help me?"

"Certainly," said the tree. "What do you want me to do?"

"Let me climb into your branches, and when the water rises enough to catch me, grow another length to get away from it."

"Very well," said the tree, "but I can only grow another four lengths."

Manabozho scampered up the tree, getting to the top branches just as the waters of the lake began swirling around the roots of the tree. But

Manabozho was still not safe; the waters rose and rose until they were almost touching his feet.

"Little Brother!" said Manabozho to the tree, "please grow!"

And so the tree grew another length, raising Manabozho well above the flood. But this didn't last long, for the waters continued to rise quickly.

Again Manabozho asked the tree to grow, and again it grew and raised him above the flood. Still the waters rose around the tree trunk. A third time Manabozho asked the tree to grow, and the waters rose even more, threatening to reach Manabozho and drag him into the depths.

"Oh, Little Brother, please grow one last time!" said Manabozho to the tree.

The tree shot up its fourth and final length. There Manabozho closed his eyes, clung to the branches, and waited for death, but when he opened his eyes to see whether the waters were still rising, he found that they had stopped and that he was safe.

Glooscap and Uncle Turtle *(Wabanaki, Northeast Forest)*

Glooscap is the culture hero of the Wabanaki peoples from the northeastern United States and the Canadian Maritime provinces. The term "Wabanaki" does not refer to a single culture but rather to the confederacy of the Mi'kmaq, Maliseet, Passamaquoddy, Abenaki, and Penobscot peoples.

In this story, instead of fighting monsters or doing other brave deeds, Glooscap plays something of a secondary role to his old Uncle Turtle, an ugly, lazy old man. Uncle Turtle, who also is called Mikchich, acts as something of a foil to his handsome, strong young nephew. Glooscap uses his powers to turn Mikchich into a young and handsome man so that he can get a wife, but nothing Glooscap does for his uncle can change his lazy ways. Mikchich learns a hard lesson in humility and following instructions when he ends up trapped under the body of a whale that Glooscap gives him the strength to lift by himself.

There was a time when Glooscap went to Pictou to stay with his Uncle Turtle. Glooscap arrived in the village but would not stay as a guest with anyone but his old uncle. This was very disappointing for the young women of the village, for Glooscap was very strong and handsome, and they all wanted him to come and stay in their wigwams instead. "Why is that handsome young man Glooscap staying with Mikchich, that ugly old Turtle?" they complained. "It isn't fair that he should choose that lazy old man over beautiful young women like us."

But Glooscap did choose to stay with his uncle, for even though Mikchich was old and ugly and very lazy, Glooscap was fond of him and wished him well.

One day, Glooscap said to Mikchich, "Uncle, why have you never married? We should find you a wife. You shouldn't have to live here all alone."

"Bah," said Mikchich. "Who would have me, looking as I do? I may be old, but I'm not deaf, and I'm not blind. I know what the young women think about me. No, there's no point in looking, Nephew. No point at all."

"Maybe," said Glooscap, "but there is to be a great feast in the village in a few days' time. There will be many young women there. Perhaps you will find a wife at the feast."

Mikchich scoffed. "Even if I were as handsome as you, I still do not have the right clothes to wear to a feast. I'm poor, and my clothes are ragged. Everyone would still laugh at me. I'd rather stay home where I'm comfortable. You go to the feast, Nephew, and enjoy yourself. I'll just wait for you here."

Glooscap didn't really want to go to the feast himself, but he did want to help his uncle. So he said, "Uncle, what if I help you? What if I make you handsome and give you good clothes to wear? Would you go to the feast then and look for a wife?"

"If you can do that, then yes, I'd gladly go," said Mikchich, not believing that Glooscap could change him like that.

Glooscap took off his belt and handed it to his uncle. "Here, Uncle," he said, "put this on, and we'll see what follows."

Mikchich took Glooscap's belt and put it on. His skin began to smooth out and become a young man's skin. His skinny old limbs became rounded with muscle. His ugly face became very handsome. His ragged clothes changed into the finest anyone had ever seen. Soon there were two handsome young men standing in Uncle Turtle's wigwam.

"Well, look at me now!" said Mikchich. "I am certainly ready to go to the feast and to find a wife!"

Mikchich went to the feast. He entered the games and competed with all the young men. Every game he entered, he won, and all the young women were very interested indeed in this new stranger who was more handsome and stronger and more skilled than all the other young men there.

While the young women were watching Mikchich, he was watching them. He saw many beautiful women that he thought would make any man a fine wife, but his eyes kept coming back to one woman in particular. She was more beautiful than all the rest, and by the end of the day, Mikchich had his heart set on her. Mikchich went back to his wigwam and said, "Nephew, I have found the woman I want to marry. It is the youngest daughter of the chief."

"That is good!" said Glooscap. "I will go and ask her parents for you."

Glooscap took a bunch of wampum and went to the chief's wigwam. There he spoke to the young woman's parents and gave them the wampum.

"Should we let our daughter marry this Mikchich?" said the chief to his wife.

"Yes, I think he would make her a very good husband," said his wife. "I saw him at the feast, and he seems to be a fine man."

The chief called his youngest daughter to him. "We have found you a husband," he said. "Prepare a good meal, and fix up a couch for your young man."

The young woman did as her father said. She took good venison and cooked a meal, and while it was cooking, she made a couch out of the boughs of trees and covered it with a blanket of furs. When all was ready, the young woman went to Mikchich's wigwam to fetch him. The young woman brought her new husband back to her parents' wigwam, where he sat on the couch she had made and ate the meal she had prepared, and so Mikchich and the young woman were married.

Sometime after the wedding, the young woman went to Mikchich and said, "You need to go hunting. We don't have enough food. We are going to starve."

Mikchich was very lazy. He didn't want to go hunting. But his wife was insistent, so he left the wigwam, thinking that he would walk around for a while and then go home and tell his wife he hadn't been able to catch anything. During his walk, he went down by the seashore, where he found some of the men trying to pull a whale they had caught up to the village. "Aha!" thought Mikchich. "I know how to make my wife think I am a good hunter and a good husband, and it will be easy."

Mikchich went to his nephew, Glooscap. He explained that he wanted to bring the whale home so that he could show his wife what a good provider he could be. Glooscap listened carefully to his uncle and then said, "All right. I'll give you the strength to move the whale all by yourself. But don't take it any farther than your father-in-law's wigwam!"

Mikchich went down to the beach, where the men were still struggling to pull the whale ashore. "I can help with that!" said Mikchich. "I'll take it up to the village myself."

The other men laughed. "If we can't even pull this great beast onto the beach when twenty of us are working, how do you think you'll fare carrying it by yourself?"

Mikchich insisted, so the men let him try, thinking that at the very least they would be able to laugh at Mikchich's efforts. They didn't laugh long, for Mikchich waded into the surf and put his shoulders under the whale. He gave one great heave and put the whale on his back. Then he started walking back to the village, carrying the whale all by himself, while the other men of the village stared in disbelief.

"This is easy!" said Mikchich. "Why should I stop at the chief's wigwam? I'll take this all the way to my own place, and my wife will see what a mighty hunter I am, and so will all the men! We'll see who's laughing when I'm done with this."

This was a big mistake. Because Mikchich was thinking about how wonderful he was and how everyone would be envious of him, and how he would do even more than Glooscap told him to do, Mikchich stumbled on his way into the village, and the whale came crashing down on top of him. The people all gathered round the whale, wondering what to do. Soon Glooscap arrived.

"Your uncle is underneath the whale!" cried the people. "He stumbled when he was carrying it, and now he is crushed flat! What should we do?"

Glooscap laughed. "My uncle will be fine," he said. "Just cut up the whale right here, and bring the pieces back to the village."

The villagers did what Glooscap said. They cut up the whale and brought it back to the village, where they prepared a great feast. When the food was all cooked and the people were all sitting and eating and enjoying themselves, who should wander into the village but Mikchich, looking none the worse for the wear!

Mikchich realized the people were staring at him. "Oh, don't mind me," he said, "I was just taking a nap on the beach."

And to this day, turtles have flat shells because of how Uncle Turtle was crushed by the whale.

Brave Woman *(Hunkpapa Sioux, Great Plains)*

Some Indigenous stories feature female heroes whose bravery and strength save their people from disaster or win honor for themselves and their families. The tale below, from the Hunkpapa Sioux, explains how a young woman named Brave Woman avenged the deaths of her brothers, who had been killed in battle against the Crow. Although this story is being presented in a book of myths, it is quite possible that it has a basis in historical fact.

Fighting over access to territory and food resources was common among the Plains Indians. In these battles, warriors could perform different kinds of brave acts to help their people win and also to garner personal glory for themselves. One such act was known as "counting coup," in which the warrior rode up to an enemy, touched him with a hand or a stick, and then rode away. Counting coup on an enemy gave the warrior great status, and it was considered to be an extreme disgrace to allow an enemy to count coup on oneself.

Brave Woman rides into battle not to fight and kill but to count coup, in order to bring disgrace on the warriors who killed her brothers. Although Brave Woman's father is saddened by her desire to ride into battle, he does not try to stop her. Instead, he grants her the honor of carrying his own coup stick and wearing his own eagle-feather war bonnet into the fray.

This story is based on a version told by Jenny Leading Cloud, a member of the Rosebud Reservation in South Dakota.

Long, long ago, before the white people came to what is now Minnesota, there lived a chief of the Hunkpapa Sioux named *Tawa Makoce*, or "His Country." He was a great warrior in his prime and a very wise leader. His people trusted and honored him. His Country had four children: three sons and one daughter. The daughter was called *Winyan Ohitika*, which means "Brave Woman."

Now, at that time, the Hunkpapa were often at war with the Crow tribe. The Hunkpapa and the Crow fought a great many battles, and when His Country's sons were old enough, they went to war, hoping to prove themselves and to live up to their great father's example. But His Country's sons did not share their father's good fortune. One by one, the three young men were killed in battles against the Crow, and soon of His Country's four children only Brave Woman was left.

Brave Woman was very beautiful. Many young men wanted to have her for a wife, but every time a young man's father went to ask her to be a bride for his son, Brave Woman refused. It did not matter how handsome the young man was or how many horses the young man's family offered as dowry. Brave Woman would not agree to marry any of them. To each one, she said, "All my brothers have fallen in battle against the Crow. I will not marry until I have gone out to battle myself to avenge their deaths."

There came a time when the Crow tried to take more territory along the Upper Missouri River, territory that the Hunkpapa considered to be their own. The Hunkpapa mounted a war party to go after the Crow and make them retreat from the area they had just taken. Among the war party were two young men who had vied for Brave Woman's hand. One was named Red Horn, and the other was Little Eagle. Red Horn was the son of a chief, and his father had tried many, many times to get Brave Woman to agree to marry his son. But Little Eagle was from a poor family, and even though he loved Brave Woman very much, he was never able to get up the courage to ask for her hand himself.

When Brave Woman saw that a war party was going out to confront the Crow, she saw that her time for vengeance had come. She put on her best clothing and took up her brothers' weapons. She readied her father's best horse. Then she went to her father and said, "Father, the time has come for me to go and count coup against the Crow. The time has come for me to avenge my brothers. Please don't try to stop me; this is something I must do."

"My daughter, you are my only remaining child. I wish you would stay home with me. But I know how strong is your desire, and it is a good desire. You may go, with my blessing. Here is my war bonnet. Wear it proudly. Do what you must do."

Brave Woman put on her father's war bonnet. She mounted her pony and went to join the war party. At first, the warriors were surprised to see her, but they did not ask her to leave. Brave Woman went to Red Horn. "Take my eldest brother's lance and shield," she said. "Count coup for him with them." Then she went to Little Eagle and said "Take my middle brother's bow and arrows. Count coup for him with them." Brave Woman gave her youngest brother's war club to another warrior. For herself, she kept her father's own coup stick.

The war party came across a Crow encampment and rode down to attack. Brave Woman did not go with the first charge; she stayed back and sang war songs and made the war cry that Sioux women make to encourage their men while they fight. Soon it became clear that the Hunkpapa were unlikely to succeed. They were greatly outnumbered by the Crow, and as the Crow pushed the Hunkpapa war party back, Brave Woman spurred her pony and rode into the fray. Brave Woman did not try to injure or kill the Crow warriors. Instead, she touched them with her father's coup stick, counting coup for her dead brothers. When the Hunkpapa warriors saw how courageously Brave Woman rode here and there among the Crow, they rallied, and for a while it seemed they might drive the enemy back.

But the press of Crow warriors was too great. The Hunkpapa were driven back again. Suddenly, Brave Woman's pony lurched and went down. He had been killed by a musket shot. Red Horn saw Brave Woman fall. He rode past her without so much as looking at her, and Brave Woman disdained to ask him for help. A moment later, Little Eagle galloped over to where Brave Woman was standing. He dismounted and asked her to get on his pony.

Brave Woman mounted the pony and waited for Little Eagle to join her. "You have to go alone," said Little Eagle. "My pony was wounded in the battle. He won't be able to carry both of us safely."

"I can't leave you here on foot!" said Brave Woman. "The Crow will surely kill you."

For answer, Little Eagle took Brave Woman's brother's bow and slapped the pony on the rump with it. The pony bolted and carried Brave Woman away from the battle. Little Eagle himself went back into the battle to help his war party.

When Brave Woman was able to get control of the pony, she went back to the battle as well. There she rallied all the Hunkpapa warriors, and they were so roused by her courage and fury that they beat back the Crow, despite their overwhelming numbers. The Crow had to admit defeat, and so they left the Upper Missouri.

The Hunkpapa were grateful for their victory, but they also mourned for all the warriors who had fallen in the battle. Among the fallen was Little Eagle, who had so bravely helped his friend. Red Horn was scorned for leaving Brave Woman to die. His bow was broken, and he was sent back to his own people.

The Hunkpapa took Little Eagle's body to the place where the Crow had been encamped. There they erected a scaffold high above the ground and placed Little Eagle upon it. They killed his pony underneath the scaffold so that he might continue to serve Little Eagle in the afterlife.

Back in the Hunkpapa camp, Brave Woman slashed her forearms and cut her hair. She tore her fine robe. She did all these things to show that she mourned for Little Eagle. For the rest of her life, she refused to marry anyone and asked that she be treated as though she were Little Eagle's widow. The people honored her request from that moment on.

Blood Clot Boy *(Ute, Great Basin)*

The buffalo was one of the most important sources of food, clothing, and shelter for the peoples of the Great Plains and the Great Basin in the western United States. It is no surprise, then, that the buffalo also figures largely in the storytelling of these cultures.

Blood Clot is a culture hero associated particularly with the buffalo, and is held in common by many tribes from the Plains and the Basin. In this story from the Ute people, Blood Clot has a miraculous birth from a clot of buffalo blood that is placed in a kettle to be made into soup for two elderly people who are starving. That Blood Clot is a supernatural being is confirmed by his prodigious growth; it only takes a few days for him to reach physical maturity, after which he shows supernatural prowess in hunting that it is dangerous for others to witness.

As is the way with such beings, Blood Clot does not spend much time among ordinary humans. When Blood Clot's wife breaks the taboo against saying the word "calf" in her husband's hearing, Blood Clot flees the encampment of the people and turns into a buffalo, in which shape he roams the prairies ever after.

A long time ago, there lived a very old man and his wife. Life was very difficult for them. The old man tried his best to hunt to bring back food, but they lived in a place where game was very scarce, and so they often went hungry.

One day the old man went out to hunt. As he walked along, he noticed a set of buffalo tracks. The old man's heart rose. If he could get just one buffalo, he and his wife would eat well for a long time! They could feast on fresh meat tonight and dry the rest for later.

The old man followed the tracks carefully, but the only thing he found was a large blood clot on the ground. He picked up the clot gently, folded it in his shirt, and went home, where he gave the clot to his wife to cook. The old woman put the blood clot in a pot with some water and set it over the fire, but when the pot began to steam, suddenly there were cries coming from inside the pot! The old man went to the pot and looked inside. Instead of the blood clot, there was a small baby boy, waving his fists and crying. The old man took the boy out of the pot. The old woman bathed him and wrapped him in warm clothes, and soon the baby had gone to sleep.

In the morning, the old couple was surprised to find that the baby had grown in the night. He continued to grow throughout the day. By sunset, he was big and strong enough to crawl about. The next day, he was trying to stand up, and the day after that, he began to walk by himself. The old couple named the boy "Blood Clot," and they raised him as their son.

Soon Blood Clot was big enough to go out hunting. His father made him a bow and arrows, and every day Blood Clot would hunt and return with something for the family to eat. Sometimes he caught a rabbit. Sometimes he caught a deer. Other times he brought home birds. But he never came home empty-handed, and the old couple rejoiced that they were never hungry anymore.

One day, when Blood Clot had grown into the stature of a young man, he went to his parents and said, "I would like to go and find another village and meet new people. I will not leave you hungry; I am going to go hunt now and will hunt all day and all night. You need to stay inside the tipi. Weight the edges down with rocks, and close the door securely so that the tipi won't blow away. No matter how the wind may howl, you must stay inside. I will call you when you can come out."

The old couple did what their son instructed. They spent the day inside the tipi, but all was quiet. At sunset, they went to sleep and slept soundly until daybreak when the sound of a loud wind began to rush all around their home.

"I must go and see what this whirlwind is," said the old man, but his wife said, "No! We must stay inside as Blood Clot told us to do."

The old man stayed inside, and he and his wife shivered in fear as the wind roared and roared around their home and shook the tipi. Suddenly, the wind stopped, and they heard Blood Clot calling to them. "Mother! Father! You can come outside now!" he said.

The old couple left the tipi and gaped in astonishment. All around their home were dozens of dead buffalo. "I have killed all of these for you," said Blood Clot. "You can dry the meat and cure the hides. This will last you a long, long time. Soon I must be on my way. Mother, will you pack a little food for me to take with me?"

"Yes, my son," said the old woman. She packed him some pemmican to take with him while he readied himself for the journey. When all was ready, Blood Clot said goodbye to his parents and set out to find a village with many new people for him to meet. He wore his best buckskin breeches and brought with him his best bow and a fine quiver of arrows.

After a few days, Blood Clot came across a village of people. He went to one of the people who lived at the edge of the camp and asked where he might find the chief. The man told Blood Clot that the chief's lodge was in the center of the camp. Blood Clot went to the lodge. There he found the chief and his daughter sitting together outside.

"Welcome," said the chief. "Sit down with us. Tell us your name and who your people are."

Blood Clot thanked the chief and sat down. "My name is Blood Clot, but I don't know who my people are. I am here to visit with you."

The chief invited the other villagers to come and meet their new visitor. Everyone came to the chief's lodge, even though they were weak with hunger from lack of game. When everyone was gathered, the chief said, "This young man is called Blood Clot. He says he doesn't know who his people are. Maybe one of us knows?"

"Are you from the Deer people?" asked one. Blood Clot said that he thought not.

"What about the Otter people?" asked another.

"No, that doesn't sound right either," said Blood Clot.

The people listed tribe after tribe, but none of them sounded right to Blood Clot until an old man said, "Maybe you are one of the Buffalo people. As I look at you here, I feel that you are of the Buffalo tribe."

Blood Clot thought about this for a moment, then agreed that this sounded right. The people of the village liked Blood Clot very much. They asked him to stay in their village, and soon they asked him whether he would like to marry the chief's daughter. Blood Clot agreed, and the young people were wed.

On the evening of the wedding, Blood Clot went to his father-in-law and said, "Please bring me one arrow from your tipi. Then tell all the people in the village to put rocks at the bottom of their tipis to hold them down, and to tie the doors shut securely. You should do the same with your tipi. Around daybreak, you will hear the noise of a great whirlwind, but you all must stay inside. I will let you know when it is safe to come out."

The chief and the villagers did as Blood Clot instructed, and at daybreak they heard the noise of a strong wind blowing through their camp. It shook the tipis, and the people were frightened, but they stayed inside until the wind stopped and they heard Blood Clot calling to them.

"Come outside!" said Blood Clot. "I have something good to show you!"

The people came out of their tipis and gasped in astonishment. At the door of every tipi in the village, there was a dead buffalo. The people dressed the buffalo and prepared some of the meat for a great feast. The rest they dried to use later, and they prepared the hide and bones and organs in their traditional ways to use for tools and clothing and other needful things.

At the feast, Blood Clot told his wife, "Because I am of the Buffalo people, you must never say the word 'calf' in my hearing. The Buffalo Calf is part of who I am, and you must not say that word."

Blood Clot lived happily with his wife in her village for a long time. But then one day a herd of buffalo was passing close to the village. Blood Clot and the other hunters went out and killed many fine buffalo. While the people of the village were skinning and dressing the dead animals, another herd of buffalo passed very close to the village. At the outer edge of the herd was a fine young calf. Blood Clot's wife saw it, and forgetting what her husband had told her, she shouted, "Kill that calf!"

As soon as Blood Clot heard his wife's shout, he jumped on his horse and rode toward the buffalo. Blood Clot's wife ran after him, crying and shouting for him to come back, but to no avail. As Blood Clot entered the herd, he began to change form, and soon he was a buffalo himself. Blood Clot never returned to his village. From that time on, he remained a buffalo and ran with his herd.

Check out more mythology books by Matt Clayton

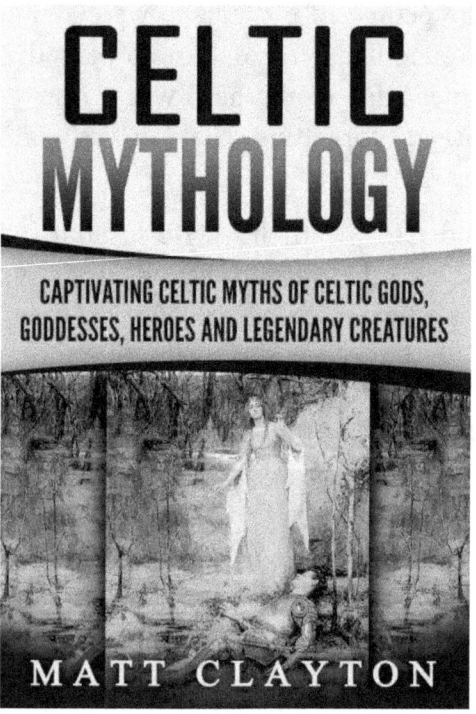

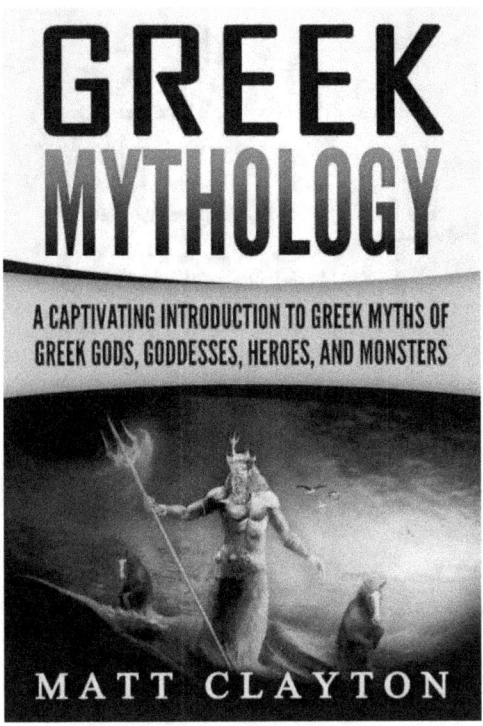

Bibliography

Indigenous Myths and Legends

Albert, Roy, et al. *Coyote Tales (English Version)*. Flagstaff: North Arizona Supplementary Education Center, 1970.

Arkansas Archeological Survey. "Story 4: Coyote and the Origins of Death." *Indians of Arkansas*. <archeology.uark.edu/indiansofarkansas/index.html?pageName=Story 4: Coyote and the Origins of Death> Accessed 9 August 2019.

Barrett, Samuel Alfred. "Pomo Myths." *Bulletin of the Public Museum of the City of Milwaukee* 15 (1933): 1-608.

———. *Myths of the Southern Sierra Miwok*. Berkeley: University of California Press, 1919.

Bayliss, Clara K. *A Treasury of Eskimo Tales*. New York: Thomas Y. Crowell Company, 1922.

Bierhorst, John. *The Mythology of North America*. New York: William Morrow and Company, 1985.

Bloomfield, Leonard. *Menomini Texts*. New York: G. E. Stechert, 1928.

Clark, Ella E. *Indian Legends of the Pacific Northwest*. Berkeley: University of California Press, 1953.

Curtis, Natalie. "Creation Myth of the Cochans (Yuma)." *The Craftsman* 16 (1909): 559-67.

DeArmond, Dale. *The Boy who Found the Light*. San Francisco: Sierra Club Books, 1990.

Dorsey, George A. *Traditions of the Caddo*. Washington, D. C.: Carnegie Institution of Washington, 1905.

Erdoes, Richard, and Alfonso Ortiz, eds. *American Indian Myths and Legends*. New York: Pantheon Books, 1984.

⸺. *The Sound of Flutes and other Indian Legends*. New York: Pantheon Books, 1976.

Gifford, Edward Winslow, and Gwendoline Harris Block. *Californian Indian Nights Entertainment*. Glendale: Arthur H. Clark Company, 1930.

Huffstetler, Edward W. *Myths of the World: Tales of Native America*. New York: Metro Books, 1996.

Judson, Katharine Berry. *Myths and Legends of British North America*. Chicago: A. C. McClurg & Co. 1917.

⸺. *Myths and Legends of California and the Old Southwest*. Chicago: A. C. McClurg & Company, 1912.

⸺. *Myths and Legends of Alaska*. Chicago: A. C. McClurg & Co., 1911.

⸺. *Myths and Legends of the Pacific Northwest*. Chicago: A. C. McClurg & Co., 1910.

Kroeber, Alfred L. "Cheyenne Tales." *Journal of American Folk-Lore* 13 (1900): 161-90.

Latta, Frank Forrest. *California Indian Folklore*. Self-published, Shafter, California, 1936.

Leeming, David Adam. *Creation Myths of the World: An Encyclopedia*. 2nd ed. Volume 1: Parts I and II. Santa Barbara: ABC-CLIO, 2010.

———, and Jake Page. *The Mythology of Native North America*. Norman: University of Oklahoma Press, 1998.

———, and Margaret Leeming. *A Dictionary of Creation Myths*. Oxford: Oxford University Press, 1994.

Leland, Charles G. *The Algonquin Legends of New England: or, Myths and Folk Lore of the Micmac, Passamaquoddy, and Penobscot Tribes*. Boston: Houghton, Mifflin and Company, 1884.

Malotki, Ekkehart. *Gullible Coyote/Una'ihu: A Bilingual Collection of Hopi Coyote Stories*. Tucson: University of Arizona Press, 1985.

Mayer, Marianna. *Women Warriors: Myths and Legends of Heroic Women*. New York: Morrow Junior Books, 1999.

Mechling, W. H. *Malecite Tales*. Ottawa: Government Printing Bureau, 1914.

Millman, Lawrence. *A Kayak Full of Ghosts*. Santa Barbara: Capra Press, 1987.

Morris, Cora. *Stories from Mythology: North American*. Boston: Marshall Jones Company, 1924.

Powers, Stephen. *Tribes of California*. Contributions to North American Ethnology, vol. 3. Washington, D. C.: Government Printing Office, 1877.

Prince, John Dyneley. *Passamaquoddy Texts*. New York: G. E. Stechert & Co., 1921.

Rasmussen, Knud. *Eskimo Folk-Tales*. Trans. and ed. W. Worster. London: Gylendal, 1921.

Schomp, Virginia. *Myths of the World: The Native Americans*. New York: Marshall Cavendish Benchmark, 2008.

Sekaquaptewa, Emory, and Barbara Pepper, ed. and trans. *Coyote and Little Turtle/Iisaw Niqw Yöngösonhoya: A Traditional Hopi Tale*. Based on a story told by Herschel Talashoema. Santa Fe: Clear Light Publishers, 1994.

Spence, Lewis. *The Myths of the North American Indians*. London: G. Harrap, 1914.

Swann, Brian, ed. *Algonquian Spirit: Contemporary Translations of the Algonquian Literatures of North America*. Lincoln: University of Nebraska Press, 2005.

Teit, James Alexander. *Memoir of the American Museum of Natural History, New York*. Vol. 2, pt. 7: *The Shuswap*. Leiden: E. J. Brill, Ltd., 1909.

Thompson, Stith. *Tales of the North American Indians*. Cambridge, MA: Harvard University Press, 1929.

Tigerman, Kathleen, ed. *Wisconsin Indian Literature: Anthology of Native Voices*. Madison: University of Wisconsin Press, 2006.

Wilson, Gilbert L. *Indian Hero Tales*. New York: American Book Company, 1916.

General Background

Childs, Craig. *Atlas of a Lost World: Travels in Ice Age America*. New York: Pantheon Books, 2018.

Culin, Stewart. "Games of the North American Indians." In *Twenty-Fourth Annual Report of the Bureau of American Ethnology of the Smithsonian Institution*, pp. 1-

846. Washington, D. C.: Government Printing Office, 1907.

Gugliotta, Guy. "When Did Humans Come to the Americas?" Smithsonian.com, February 2013. <https://www.smithsonianmag.com/science-nature/when-did-humans-come-to-the-americas-4209273/>.

Worrall, Simon. "When, How Did the First Americans Arrive? It's Complicated." *National Geographic,* 9 June 2018. <https://www.nationalgeographic.com/news/2018/06/when-and-how-did-the-first-americans-arrive--its-complicated-/>.

www.ingramcontent.com/pod-product-compliance
Lightning Source LLC
Chambersburg PA
CBHW062052280426
43661CB00088B/824